'A Small Room in Clarges Street'

Secret War-Time Lectures
at the Royal Central Asian Society, 1942–1944

'A Small Room in Clarges Street'

Secret War-Time Lectures
at the Royal Central Asian Society, 1942–1944

Edited by Rosie Llewellyn-Jones

sussex
ACADEMIC
PRESS
Brighton • Chicago • Toronto

2 4 6 8 10 9 7 5 3 1

First published in 2014 by
SUSSEX ACADEMIC PRESS
PO Box 139
Eastbourne BN24 9BP

and in the United States of America by
SUSSEX ACADEMIC PRESS
Independent Publishers Group
814 N. Franklin Street, Chicago, IL 60610

and in Canada by
SUSSEX ACADEMIC PRESS (CANADA)
1108 / 115 Antibes Drive, Toronto, Ontario M2R 2Y9

British Library Cataloguing in Publication Data
A CIP catalogue record for this book is available from the British Library.

Library of Congress Cataloging-in-Publication Data
"A small room in Clarges Street" : secret war-time lectures at the Royal Central Asian Society, 1942–1944 / [edited by] Rosie Llewellyn-Jones.
pages cm
Includes bibliographical references and index.
ISBN 978-1-84519-633-2 (hardback : acid-free paper)
1. Middle East—Politics and government—1945–1979. 2. Soviet Union—Politics and government—1945–1991. 3. Social change—Middle East—History—20th century. 4. Social change—Soviet Union—History. 5. Middle East—Foreign relations—Great Britain. 6. Soviet Union—Foreign relations—Great Britain. 7. Great Britain—Foreign relations—Middle East. 8. Great Britain—Foreign relations—Soviet Union. 9. Royal Central Asian Society—Records and correspondence. 10. Lectures and lecturing—England—London. I. Llewellyn-Jones, Rosie. II. Royal Central Asian Society.
DS63.1.S595 2014
940.53—dc23

2013046105

Typeset and designed by Sussex Academic Press, Brighton & Eastbourne.
Printed by TJ International, Padstow, Cornwall.
This book is printed on acid-free paper.

Contents

Foreword

The Royal Society for Asian Affairs (the Royal Central Asian Society at the time of the articles in this collection) possesses a small but rich archive. Over recent years much has been done to organise and catalogue it, not least with the thankful aid of voluntary helpers. A catalogue is now available in both the Society office and the National Archives:
(http://www.nationalarchives.gov.uk/a2a/records.aspx?cat=3068-rsaa_2-2&cid=-1#-1)

Although I was Chairman of the Society for some years I was quite unaware of the existence of the treasure trove of articles from the 1940s that Rosie Llewellyn-Jones has unearthed. She deserves our warm thanks not only for the work of research but also for writing an introduction to them that is so comprehensive that it leaves little to be said in a Foreword.

The ten articles are of various types. Seven are focussed on the Middle East; three on the Soviet Union. Two are by authors whose names later became household words in academe – Hamilton Gibb and Albert Hourani: most are by Army or Royal Air Force officers. Some give a close-up view of current events, for example the Rashid Ali revolt in Iraq in 1941, the resistance of the Red Army to the Nazi invasion, or – written with a remarkable lack of rancour – what it was like to be an exiled Polish noblewoman in Kazakh Siberia. Some on the other hand are wide-ranging, discussing for example post-war relations between Britain and the Middle East, Arab nationalism, and Arab unity. One article is devoted to the Assyrians, the sad substance of which prompts the thought that it has generally been, as it remains today, an uncertain business to belong to a minority in the Middle East.

All the articles are written in clear English, are relevant to the time in which they were written, but also offer thoughtful pointers, accurate or not as they might turn out to be, to the future. A sentence that particularly resonated with me was written by the RAF author of the first article in the collection, writing of Basra in 1938: "I discovered that British officials and people like myself . . . , although we were reasonably popular individually, were regarded with very great suspicion as a class". My experience too, over a career spent largely in the Arab world, has been that while Arab people have been very ready to be friendly with British people, they have in general cordially detested the policies of the British government.

I like to think that the Society of today, in its lectures and its journal *Asian Affairs*, and in the voluntary contributions of its members backing up a tiny dedicated staff, is maintaining the same high standards exemplified in *A Small Room in Clarges Street*.

Sir Harold Walker
23 January 2014

List of Illustrations

Cover
Clarges Street, Mayfair. Artist: Geoffrey Fletcher. Copyright: The Estate of the Artist. Image: courtesy the Totteridge Gallery, Earls Colne, Essex.

Plate section (after page 94)

Map (page 158)
The German Front in Russia, 1941 (Graphics: Jane Booker Nielsen)

'STRICTLY CONFIDENTIAL'

Introduction

In January 1942 Major Edward Ainger, the Honorary Treasurer of the Royal Central Asian Society[1] made an innovative suggestion at the first Council meeting of the new year. He pointed out that the Society's lectures, which had continued to be held during the war, dealt only with current events, or 'situations already in being' as he put it. He suggested that it might be useful to look further ahead – to a time when the war would be over – to examine probable trends and how to deal with them. In particular he wanted to examine the 'general attitude of Asiatics to Europeans, more especially the British . . . ' Such an examination, he thought, might foster trade and prevent mistakes in the future, if it were done now. Like a number of the Society's officers, Ainger had a military background and had worked as an interpreter in Russian and Japanese, retiring from the Army in 1937 as Brigade-Major in Shanghai.

It was the economic implications of the Atlantic Charter, agreed between Britain and America, that had prompted Ainger's statement. The Charter was drawn up in August 1941 by Winston Churchill, wartime prime minister, and Franklin Roosevelt, president of the United States of America. It was an ambitious and aspirational document that declared, among other things, that 'all people had a right to self-determination;' that trade barriers were to be lowered and that there was to be global economic co-operation. How this was to be achieved was not spelled out, and arguments arose between Churchill and Roosevelt as to whether the Charter's proposals covered only countries liberated from the grip of the Axis powers or whether it had world-wide application. If it was to have an international dimension, then how would Britain's Indian Empire and her many colonies be affected?

While the implications of the Charter were still being debated, the Society was looking ahead and wanted 'suitable lecturers' to discuss the probable trends of post-war major economic developments, political and cultural changes and conflicts likely to arise if the Charter was implemented. The Society's object was 'to study the type of education required to enable our official and commercial representatives to interpret Anglo-American experience into local terms'. This was by no means just a theoretical exercise. The Society counted among its members and friends a highly influential group of government advisors, diplomats, military officers, civil servants, explorers, educationalists and even journalists.

The guest list for the Society's sherry party in October 1941 included two Ambassadors (Egypt and Turkey), five Ministers (Netherlands, Afghanistan, Nepal, Saudi Arabia, Thailand), representatives from the Iraq Legation, the Chinese Embassy, and the Indian High Commission; the Secretary of State for India (Leo Amery), the Colonial Office Under-Secretary, the President of the British Council, staff from the British Museum, the School of Oriental & African Studies, the BBC and Dr Chaim Weizman, who was to become the first President of Israel seven years later.[2] The Society, almost from its inception in 1901, had been pressing government to establish an 'Oriental School of Learning' in London and when the School of Oriental Studies[3] finally opened in 1916, its first director was Sir Denison Ross, who was a Council member and then Vice-President of the Society. So Major Ainger's suggestion that lectures and discussions at the Society, during the darkest days of the war, would inform post-war British policy and commercial ventures abroad was not an idle boast.

Finding suitable lecturers was a problem. The Society's Council, meeting on 10 July 1942, a day after the first lecture in this book was given, complained that it was 'exceedingly difficult to get good lectures in War time and also the people were anxious to hear what was of interest at the minute'. It was agreed that the responsibility for a plan of lectures should be given to three members of Council. The areas to be covered were the Far East, the Middle East and the Near East. Of the lectures published here, seven are on the Middle East. Some of the original foolscap typescripts, scanned for this book, are marked 'Private and Confidential' and the audience was warned by the Chairman that the lectures were not to be discussed outside the lecture room. A member of the audience for the lecture on 'Post-war Britain and the Middle East', given in January 1943, was the Chairman of the Joint Intelligence Committee, Harold Caccia (later Sir Harold). He took part in the discussion but prefaced his remarks, saying 'it is against the general rule of my Office . . . to be allowed to address a meeting at all, and I have only obtained a somewhat reluctant approval for saying a few words today, so that I would beg that anything I may say should be regarded as strictly confidential and should not be quoted as the views of the Foreign Office, or quoted indeed at all.'

The apparent anomaly of discussing post-war policy, and eye-witness accounts from sensitive areas of the Middle East, and Russia but at the same time keeping it all secret, was circumvented by selecting the audience in advance. The matter was raised in March

1943, when a Council member said he had not realised that only 'special members' received invitation cards to these confidential lectures. Wouldn't this alienate the Society's ordinary members, particularly if non-members had been invited? A lively discussion evidently took place. Colonel Stewart Newcombe, who was responsible for the Middle East lectures, spoke strongly in favour of restricting the 'special meetings to those who were able to contribute something of value to the discussion', and he did not object to non-members with specialist knowledge being invited over ordinary members. He admitted that protests had been received from the Society's members who had objected to being left out. However, he argued, the room for the special meetings was small and there was a great difference between the discussions held at these meetings and those held in a hall. Perhaps the special meetings could be looked on as 'study circles?' It was agreed that no change should be made, and the Secretary offered to go through the regional index of members, adding such names 'as he thought advisable' and leaving out such as he considered would not be of use.

Because of the confidential nature of the lectures, the discussions that followed, the selected and select audience, and the ingrained wartime habit of secrecy, only one of the lectures was published in the Society's Journal – 'A Forecast of Arab Unity' by Colonel Newcombe himself, although the interesting discussion that followed his talk was not printed. The lectures were found randomly in the Society's archives in 2012. In one case the name of the secretarial bureau that provided short-hand writers is given, and we assume that the lectures were taken down verbatim, then typed up. This gives them an authentic air of spontaneity, particularly in the discussions that followed, and one can imagine the sometimes heated, although always courteous, atmosphere in the small room in Clarges Street, London, W1 where most of the lectures took place at lunch time.

The importance of these lectures is that they cover places and events generally neglected by conventional histories of World War Two. The three main arenas of war were Europe and European Russia; the Far East, particularly after the fall of Singapore in 1942, and north Africa. Only one lecture in this book 'German and Russian Armies', given in 1944 by General Sir Giffard le Quesne Martel, an engineer, discusses a topic that would have been familiar to the general public – the successful resistance of the Soviet Red Army to the Nazi invasion. The other two lectures in the Russia Section are on subjects then completely unknown even to the invited audience – what it was like to be in Moscow shortly after the Nazi invasion; and a first-hand account of life in Siberia by an exiled Polish noblewoman.

The lectures in the Middle East Section take us into a world which is simultaneously both painfully familiar and yet extraordinarily remote. The continuing upheavals in the so-called Arab world (a loose term that often, inaccurately, includes Iran) have their origins in the dismantling of the vast Ottoman Empire at the end of World War One. During its six-hundred-year long existence, countries within the Empire had varying degrees of autonomy and while some were willing participants, others fought to disengage themselves, sometimes with foreign assistance. The Ottoman Empire, like other unions of disparate countries, always contained within itself the potential for disintegration. There was, after all, little in common between the sophisticated citizens of its capital, Constantinople, and the desert dwellers around the mud-brick town of Al-Diriyah in the Nejd, the furthest, and disputed, outpost of Empire. By the late nineteenth century, Turkey was being described as 'the sick man of Europe.'[4] Its support for Germany, its massacres of ethnic minorities including Armenians and Assyrians, and its subsequent defeat in the first world war, led to the Empire being partitioned among the victors, initially by the Treaty of Sèvres (1920) and later by the Treaty of Lausanne (1923). Countries within the former Empire were divided up among Britain and France, who were given a mandate (a legal obligation) to rule them. Britain got Mesopotamia (subsequently known as Iraq[5]) and Palestine, while France got Syria and the Lebanon.

Britain already had a substantial foothold in Mesopotamia, having initially sent in troops in 1914 to protect the oil refinery at Abadan. The link between oil and European intervention thus goes back a century. With the help of the 6th Poona Division, the British Indian Expeditionary Force moved northwards, overcoming Ottoman resistance, and in 1917 entered Baghdad, where the British were greeted as liberators. The Ottomans were expelled, but Iraqi hopes of independence were dashed when Britain brought in civil servants from India and set up a provisional government, based heavily on its administration of India.[6] The first British High Commissioner for Iraq was Sir Percy Cox and eighteen British advisers were attached to the novice ministries. Of this group no fewer than nine were members of the Central Asian Society,[7] including H. St. John Philby, and the High Commissioner himself.

The coastal country of Lebanon was carved out of what had been Greater Syria, and was part of the French mandate. Syria itself was divided up into States, which reflect fairly accurately the different tribal regions, with the Alawis to the north-west and the Druze to the south east. This at least was a recognition that the Ottoman Empire was made up not just of countries, but more importantly, of tribes, with their loyalty to clan leaders, and their frequent antipathy to other tribes. Further divisions arose from religious beliefs – Sunnis, Shi'as, Christians of all sects and Jews formed a rich but potentially explosive mixture. The Kurds, largely Sunni, were a migratory tribe spread across Turkey, Syria and Iraq and seemingly disliked by everyone.

Both Iraq and Syria tried to shake off their new masters by uprisings in the 1920s, although neither succeeded. Britain and France now had the advantage of air power and Britain took the decision to hand over control of Iraq to the newly-formed Royal Air Force, which subdued Kurdish uprisings by bombing its villages.

By the outbreak of the second world war in 1939, many elements of today's unquiet Middle East were in place. Future trends, hinted at and discussed during these war-time lectures, were to influence policy for the next half century and beyond. It is always fascinating to look back at attempts to foretell the future. The extent of American influence was certainly underestimated. Professor Gibb's lecture on 'The Middle East in American Opinion' was somewhat scornful about the USA's knowledge of the area and more so about its attitude towards a proposed Jewish homeland. No speaker anticipated the rise of Islamic fundamentalism, or the demise of the royal families of Iraq and Persia. The model of enlightened kingship presiding over pro-western kingdoms was anticipated, in spite of past evidence to the contrary. The post-war role of the Middle East Supply Centre (MESC)[8] and the British Council received positive recommendations.

'The protection of the route to India' was still of paramount strategic concern in the 1920s, at a time when it seemed inconceivable that India would not remain the 'jewel in the crown' of the British Empire. This informed much of the India Office's policy towards the Middle East, particularly as areas including the Red Sea, the Arabian Peninsula, the Gulf States, Iraq and Iran all fell at various times within its remit. But twenty years later, although it was becoming clear that post-war, the relationship between Britain and India would be irrevocably altered, the implications were not fully realised. More than a century of securing the Indian subcontinent against the external enemy (Russia) and internal dissension, had produced a mindset that found it difficult, if not impossible, to imagine the day when Britain's business with India would be finished. There would be no more need to patrol the sea-route to India, neither would there be Indian troops to fight Britain's battles, nor administrators to set up new governments in the Middle East.

Although so much has changed today, current events give many of these seventy-year old lectures a peculiar poignancy and relevance. The world in which they were delivered, in war-time London, is very different from today, yet many of the seeds of today's conflicts were examined here, all those years ago. As for the Russia lectures, the eye-witness accounts form a valuable, historic document of no less interest. The words of the lecturers and the audience speak for themselves, so there has been minimal editing, and introductions to each chapter.

Notes

1 Now The Royal Society for Asian Affairs.
2 The total cost of the sherry party was £26. 16s. 5d, including 'Harrods, for Service and Hire'.
3 The School of Oriental Studies became the School of Oriental & African Studies (SOAS) in 1936.
4 The phrase is attributed to Tsar Nicholas I of Russia.
5 The name 'Iraq' is of ancient origin, and was formally adopted in 1920.
6 A detailed Report on *Iraq Administration October 1920–March 1922* was published by the British government in 1922.
7 The Central Asian Society became the Royal Central Asian Society in 1931, and the Royal Society for Asian Affairs in 1975.
8 MESC was a British organisation set up in Cairo initially to meet transport shortages (see page 75).

LECTURE ONE

Iraq 1942

By Wing Commander J.R.A. Embling, DSO, CBE
Lecture on 9 July 1942

Introduction

Between 1938 and the end of World War Two, Nazi short-wave radio broadcasts in Arabic were transmitted to the Middle East including Iraq. Summaries of the broadcasts were produced by the USA Embassy in Cairo and recent research shows how the German government presented itself as a friend of Islam and an enemy of Zionism. Hitler's propagandists told Muslims that they respected the Koran, and cited the work of German orientalists as an important sign of goodwill. It was argued that Islam and National Socialism shared goals and ideals including monotheism, obedience, discipline, self-sacrifice, courage and honour, among others. This contributed largely to the pro-German sympathies among Iraqis, reported by Embling.

Ghazi bin Faisal (1912–1939) who was born in Mecca, succeeded his father as king of Iraq in 1933. Ghazi was a pan-Arab nationalist, and opposed to British interests in his country. Britain's involvement had begun when it was given the mandate in May 1920 by the League of Nations to administer Iraq. Almost immediately Britain had to put down an Iraqi revolt with the help of bombing raids carried out by the RAF. But Britain was not without its supporters, including the prime minister Nuri al-Said. It was believed by some that he had engineered the death of Ghazi in a motoring accident in April 1939 because of the king's anti-British stance.

The fall of France in June 1940, at the start of World War Two, encouraged some Arab nationalists to turn towards Germany and Italy. Nuri al-Said lost his position as prime minister and was replaced by the pro-German Rashid Ali Al-Gaylani. Rashid Ali, as he was called, made several unsuccessful attempts to seize power for himself by capturing the prince-regent 'Abd-al-llah, who was appointed after King Ghazi's sudden death.

RAF Habbaniya was a large, self-contained British airbase on the west bank of the river Euphrates, replacing an earlier station nearer the Iraqi capital, Baghdad. Habbaniya became a training centre and staging post for aircraft at the outbreak of the war. By April 1941 the British hold on north Africa was tenuous as troops confronted the Nazi commander, Rommel. At the same time, Iraqi troops encouraged by Rashid Ali, encircled Habbaniya and from a high vantage point, began firing down at the airbase. The British retaliated with bombing raids and held out, with the help of the locally recruited Assyrian Levies, for nearly two weeks. The airbase was relieved when British troops, from India, were diverted to Iraq.

Had Habbaniya fallen to the hostile Iraqi troops, the German army in Europe, already fighting in Greece and advancing towards Crete, would have been poised to take possession of the Middle East. The British held Habbaniya and recaptured Basra, before moving on to Baghdad, but they were unable to prevent a massacre of about six hundred Jews in the capital. In January 1943 the Iraq Government, now supporting Britain, declared war on the Axis forces.

PRIVATE AND CONFIDENTIAL
ROYAL CENTRAL ASIAN SOCIETY
Report of a Private Meeting
held at 8 Clarges Street, London W1
on 9th July, 1942, at 5.30 p.m.
Chairman: Sir John Shea, GCB, KCMG, DSO
Wing-Commander J. R. A. Embling lecturing[1]

I am speaking entirely from memory and also from a rather restricted point of view of what happened out there. I was in Basra and not in Baghdad, and was concerned with a good deal of detail work, which did not allow me to take a very big view. I will not go into the details of the history of Iraq or the last twenty years with the Mandate and the eventual establishment of the kingdom of Iraq. I would like to start off from a point where I arrived at the end of 1938, when I discovered that British officials and people like myself, who were in contact with the local people, although we were reasonably popular individually, were regarded with very great suspicion as a class.

That was very largely due to German propaganda. In 1938, long before the war started, the Germans spent something like £60,000 on propaganda in Iraq directed against us. It was a rather distressing feature to find that the people who naturally one might think would be inclined to take our point of view, that is to say the officials or Army officers and so on who had been trained in England or under British officials or officers, were the worst offenders in spreading propaganda against us. [pencil note in margin: a member who knows the country well said that this was largely due to King Ghazi, he went back bitterly anti-British.[2]] That contrasted unfavourably with the people who had been to America. I think one of the reasons is that people who were educated in America were educated in technical subjects, and that when they came back to Iraq they had a career open to them, whereas officials and Army officers took the line that so long as Britain to all intents and purposes was in control of Iraq, they would not have a chance, and the Germans found it remarkably easy to work on that strain.

Then there was the particular thing which I feel strongly affected the issue, and that was that the Arab has a peculiar psychology of his own. I am inclined to put it down to what is undoubtedly present in practically all of us, to develop rather more highly trained a state, which the psychologists will recognize, of being disappointed with the world of real things as we see them, and living in a sort of dream world, grandiose schemes that are built up without any real foundation, without any conception of the hard work which is necessary to bring them into effect. In some ways this preoccupation with another world has, I think, undoubtedly been the foundation for some of the mysticism which is present among various leaders in Mohammedan religious thought, but it also works the other way. It is, I think, one of the reasons why the Arab is peculiarly liable to corruption. He starts thinking of the splendid things which he would be able to do with a sum of money or position of power, and is disinclined to regard the means by which he can achieve them. I think it also explains a remark by [T.E.] Lawrence in one of his writings to the effect that the Arab is unpredictable. He will spend a long time brooding over some project or other, and suddenly you find him in action and he goes much further than anyone would expect from his previous conduct.

That certainly happened in Iraq. The army and the local officials were to a very great extent against us. At one time it was reckoned that almost 90% of the local officials would welcome the Germans into Iraq simply for the sake of seeing the British driven out. That shows that there was a very large proportion of the people there who would have been glad to get rid of us. The army officers again, the younger ones particularly, who had had very little experience of actual fighting and who were far more concerned with their own promotion, would have been glad to see us out of the place. They knew very well the smallness of the forces we had in the country. They were frightened of air action, but I do not think they reckoned they would have to put up with very much of it. In fact, one of the Golden Four is reliably said to have told the Germans that he "was prepared to take Habbaniya in the space of seven hours."[3]

The tribespeople have now very largely lost any force they might have in the country. The Iraq police are quite competent to deal with any sort of local rising which may occur, and during the whole revolt there were only two cases of tribal action of any consequence. One of them was by Faisal,[4] who took the opportunity of the rising to pay off certain old scores on his tribal neighbours. The other was a case of one of the desert tribes, who, when the rising happened, came into Basra and offered the services of himself and his tribesmen to drive the British out of the country. The next we heard of him was a fortnight later, when he was seen leading his tribesmen on the main bazaar and looting it in the city itself.

The people who were mostly favourable to us were the larger class of merchants, particularly in Basra. There had been a movement to develop trade with Germany, and particularly with Japan. The main thing was that, after the war started, it became very difficult to get shipping to take away the products of Iraq, and the Japanese were in a very good position to guarantee export. They took the whole of the cotton crop for 1939, for instance. It was owing to this fear of the local merchants that, although we might promise to buy their goods, we would not be able to take delivery of them, that a number of the merchants were inclined to favour the Axis countries in any sort of trade developments. But the main body realized that they would drive a far better bargain with us than with the other side; they were favourably inclined towards us, but they were not prepared to take any particular action about it. I would like to go into the details of the campaigns of last year, because by going through that story, I can point out more easily how these various facts affected it.

The first thing that happened was that the Regent[5] suddenly appeared in Basra. Two months before he had to leave the capital because Rashid Ali[6] had surrounded the Regent's house with a gang of his own particular thugs and actually threatened the Regent's life if he would not fall in with Rashid's particular policy of hidden co-operation with the Germans. You must remember it was very difficult for us to prevent any contact at this time because the Italian Embassy was still in the country, and any instructions or anything else which the Germans desired to pass on to Rashid Ali could easily be done through the Italian diplomatic bag.

The Regent in February fled to Dewaniyah and there was a crisis which lasted for four or five days. The upshot was that Rashid Ali found he had not enough support in the country at that time to continue in his policy. He had to resign and Taha al-Hashimi[7] came in. The next two months was a period more or less of calm before the storm. Taha al-Hashimi had no very definite policy of his own, and then came the time when Rashid Ali thought fit to take serious steps.

You must remember that at the beginning of April [1941] we had been right up to Benghazi and been driven back again, and with a small garrison in Tobruk we were right back on the Egyptian border. At the same time the Germans had attacked and overcome Yugoslavia, and were just preparing to go into Greece and on to Crete. They had a time-table worked out, by which at the end of April they should have been able to transfer airborne troops into Syria and so across to Iraq, cutting our main line of communication by air and sea with India from the Middle East.

Rashid Ali surrounded the Regent's house a second time with his cut-throats, and it was only owing to the help of the American Ambassador that the Regent was able to get out of the house alive. He fled to Basra, but brought with him two ex-Premiers, and when he first arrived, it looked as if he had a very fair prospect of setting up an oppo-sition to the Government in power in Baghdad and maintaining himself in the country. He arrived in one of our aircraft and was conveyed into the airport hotel in Basra. He then sent for the various local army commanders and the commander of the small naval force and other people, put his plan in front of them, and that evening they aimed to carry it out. Unfortunately the army commander felt rather doubtful about his position, rang up [. . .][8] and told him the whole story, and he immediately passed it on to Baghdad. Next morning the chief of staff of the army rang up and threatened to attack with the rest of the Iraq army if the Regent were not handed over immediately. Rashid Ali decided to change sides, and sent off to capture the Regent in the airport hotel.

Fortunately we heard about this, and Sir John Ward[9] went up in his car and got the Regent away down to his own house just in time – in fact, they passed the troops on the road. It was pretty obvious that his house was not a very safe place, and it was decided to take off the party to a British gunboat which was then in the river opposite the RAF station. While they were waiting for a launch to go up the river, the troops appeared at the front gate. It was Lady Ward who saved the situation. She went out and ticked off the Iraqi officer in charge of the party for allowing the soldiers to come in and tramp down her flower garden. She told them to get out, and they did. Meanwhile the Regent and his party were getting into the launch at the other end of the lawn.

Once this had happened, it became pretty impossible to hope that any sort of Government could be constituted in Basra. The strongest of the Regent's supporters was unfortunately not able to escape. He was captured and sent up to Baghdad, and the chief of police soon followed him.

The Iraq army began moving the concentration of troops down to Basra. We had there one squadron, a very ancient aircraft Vincent, and the floating boat station at Basra with no floating boats, and one battalion of local Arab Levies. All told by the end of that week there were in the Basra district five battalions of infantry and four battalions of artillery, and it was obvious we would have no chance if we attempted to resist their demand that we give up the Regent. It was almost impossible to keep open any sort of communication with the outside. [. . .][10] hoped that by some sort of rising of his own people in the north, they might be able to do something, but obviously there were no plans prepared, and as the Iraq army had occupied the offices of our people up in the north, it was impossible to communicate with anybody up there. Our only hope was to do so by wireless, and the wireless set was confiscated as the aircraft carrying it landed at Kirkuk. The situation was pretty hopeless. At the same time we were fighting in Greece and the attack on Crete was just being prepared. It was obvious no troops could be spared from the Middle East. At first we got the same reply from India, that nothing could be spared. So it was decided to move the Regent from the country. He was taken down the river, and eventually to Transjordan.

In the meanwhile India had relented and decided that a force which was on the way to Malaya could be spared to send up to Basra. The first convoy with the Headquarters and a brigade of troops and some infantry set out. Meanwhile, Cornwallis[11] had arrived in Baghdad and took over the negotiations with Rashid Ali. At that point the situation in the Mediterranean was not sufficiently far advanced for Rashid Ali to make a complete break with us. What he was playing for was a little time in which to be recognized as the head of the Government by the British representative and to keep up his connections with the Italian Empire and the Germans. By seeing him privately and unofficially Cornwallis did manage to persuade him that, if this convoy of troops was allowed to land in Basra and the Iraqis behaved themselves, it might be possible to recognize Rashid Ali as the head of the Government. I went down to meet the convoy and we sailed up the Persian Gulf and were preparing to go up the river and get a signal from Baghdad, saying that Rashid Ali had agreed that the landing of these troops should not be resisted. The next thing was another signal, saying that the local Iraq army knew nothing about this agreement and were prepared to resist. It turned out that the people in Basra had forgotten to inform them. Eventually the convoy sailed up the river and the troops landed.

The next thing that happened was that the army in Basra prepared a camp and started to get out contracts for the supply of rations and so on, and meanwhile another convoy was on its way from India with further troops. Rashid Ali realized that he must act fairly quickly although the time-table had gone wrong. The Germans had expected to get Crete in two days. Actually it took them three weeks, and that delay of one fortnight was the saving of the whole of the Middle East in that year, because it held up the programme sufficiently for us to get enough troops into Iraq and across to Syria to prevent it being a walk over. Rashid Ali realized this was happening, and he decided that an immediate attack must be made on the forces in Iraq. So a mechanized brigade with a couple of other brigades of infantry were sent up to attack. [. . .][12] and all the British subjects in Kirkuk and everywhere else were rounded up. The people in Baghdad had time to get into the Embassy or the American Embassy, who supported something like two hundred people for a month. There were fifty in the Consulate in Baghdad.

They started off and attacked Habbaniya and then the authorities in the Middle East decided something had to be done and besides this convoy on the way from India they sent troops from Palestine across towards Habbaniya and Baghdad. With them came the Transjordan force under Colonel Glubb[13] who asked his men if they were willing to fight against their Arab brothers in Iraq. A good many were not willing. He addressed them for an hour, and at the end of that time he asked them again if they were willing, and they all fell in again, and they did excellent work. Eventually they were the most advanced of any of our troops in the country.

In Basra we had been having a very difficult time. The local army authorities had set up a special office in Basra for spying out our activities and for the definite spreading of rumours. The local people were all convinced that at any minute bombers would arrive, and the result was that nobody would go and work in the port. Our people were followed. We afterwards discovered a document in the local police force, which showed that out of thirteen plain clothes policemen employed there, four were kept on watch against myself and my colleagues, three against the British Consul, two against Mr. Lloyd, and three against another British subject, leaving one to cope with the criminal activities of the population of Basra.

Altogether things were very difficult. People were definitely prevented by the local authorities from coming to Iraq. The problem was solved for us in a way by the attack on Habbaniya, because as soon as that happened, our force in Basra naturally attacked the Iraq army there and they fired off the rounds at extraordinarily long range, both of which fell short of the two battalions of the Iraq army, which evaporated. They went upstream into the marshes and stayed there. They gave us no more trouble except for occasional raids at night.

The town of Basra was still not held by us, and the Government there was still in correspondence with Rashid Ali in Baghdad. So it was decided two days later to take over Ashur, where the Government buildings and banks were, and leave the old city, which was simply residential, to its own devices. We came down in two columns and occupied the main part of Ashur, the banks and the Government offices without any trouble. Unfortunately the Chief of Police, who had been sent down by Rashid Ali, turned out to be possibly the most anti-British person in the whole city. We discovered afterwards three telegrams from him in code, asking to be relieved of his post so that he could rejoin the army in order to fight against his deadly enemies, the British, and when our troops marched into the town he told the police to open fire, which they did. It was a very difficult situation because they held the Italian Headquarters and a considerable portion of the town with very narrow roads and tall buildings, and short of street fighting from house to house there was no way of getting them out.

What complicated it was the fact that all this had happened in the early morning, and the whole of the civil population were still in their beds. A certain amount of sporadic firing went on, and when we had occupied the main Government offices and the telephone exchange, we plugged in and rang up the Commandant of Police at the other side and asked him if he did not think it was better to stop fighting. Conversations went on, on the telephone for a couple of hours, and eventually they agreed to stop fighting and come out under a white flag. Unfortunately looting had broken out in the main bazaar between us and them, and they found they could not get out without running the gauntlet of the looters and our troops who were shooting back at the looters. So the police force eventually disappeared in the same manner as the army. They crossed the river, and those who felt like it rejoined the army higher up whilst the others changed their clothes and became part of the populace. The next day we took over the whole of Ashur, and invited the people of Basra to form a Government for themselves pending the return of the Regent.

I would like here to come back and take up the story of Habbaniya where I left off. Our camp there is in a loop of the river which forms three sides of a rectangle. In between the river and the cliffs is the aerodrome, with the camp on the far side. The Iraqi troops marched out and took up positions on this line of cliffs. They could fire down on to the aerodrome. They pitched a few shells over and managed to hit G.H.Q. a couple of times and the water tower.

All we had at the time was two-thirds of a battalion, about 2,000 airmen trained in rifle shooting and some fifty aircraft, all of which were training types. The result was that, with the aerodrome covered, it was not safe to let the people who were still only doing their training, do any flying at all, and the whole of the defence from the air and any defensive action against the Iraq army which had to be done from the air, necessarily was done by the instructors of the flying training school. I think you will appreciate the difficulties of starting up engines behind hangers, coming out between hangars and taking off right away without any preliminary taxiing, and the same thing with landing.

That went on for five days. Meanwhile, a transport squadron from India came up and flew supplies into Habbaniya, and on the return troops took out the women and children of Baghdad, who had been evacuated to Habbaniya when the trouble first boiled up. They did that without a single casualty. Eventually they were able to fly up another battalion of British troops, who went into Habbaniya and later were able to make very effective raids at night. Finally, after five days of hammering by these people from the air with the help of Wellingtons, the Iraq force decided they had had enough and they were going home.

Unfortunately they happened to meet reinforcements, which Baghdad had sent out, at a place where there was no possible way of getting off the road. Floods had broken through the year before and brought some four feet of silt across the road. These two forces met in the middle of the cutting. Our people discovered this and bombed the two ends of the cutting. That morning with the twenty or twenty-five aircraft that were left, we pushed out for 140 sorties, bombing this concentration of transport. That really disposed of the army as a formidable force. They did succeed in cutting the river bounds and flooding the country between that position and Baghdad, and they still held the town of Fallujah which had the only possible bridge for crossing the Euphrates between Syria and Basra; so it was important to get hold of that quickly and without damage to the bridge.

Our armoured brigade, which had come across from Palestine, made a further attack on their positions round the bridge head, and meanwhile we hoped for this battalion of troops. Then we landed them, and they walked into the town practically unopposed, so that the bridge was ours. It still took another fortnight to get to Baghdad, but that was mainly because the country was flooded and it was almost impossible to move any of our armoured forces.

Meanwhile, the Germans had begun to bomb and it became urgent to do something about it. Very fortunately in a bombing raid on Baghdad soon after these German machines first appeared, we happened to hit the head of the German military mission, the son of General von Schier [sic].[14] That led to confusion amongst the Germans and eased the situation for us. Some Hurricanes were sent across one evening from Palestine. The next morning the Heinkels arrived, expecting no opposition and found the Hurricanes waiting for them. As soon as that combat was over, the Hurricanes went straight off to Mosul which had become the German air base, and destroyed a large number of their machines on the ground.

Then our troops advanced up to the western limits of Baghdad. By this time Rashid Ali realized that he could get no valuable support from the Germans. Their help from the air had not been very effective, and it was found that their timetable had been badly upset, and he decided it was time to get out. So he and the four members of the military Golden Square left Baghdad with a month's pay for the army and went off towards Persia. Fortunately there was an alert customs man on the frontier who took the month's pay from them.

Baghdad was left without any Government for the time being, which was a most unfortunate thing, because the hooligans of Rashid Ali's following and the Youth Movement, boys of fifteen or sixteen, who had been armed by Rashid Ali, got out of hand and started a massacre in the Jewish quarter, and a tremendous number of Jews were killed, something like two thousand, in a very few hours.[15] The only thing that stopped it was an Iraqi General, who gathered together what troops he could and ordered them into the streets to shoot anybody carrying a bundle. That soon had an effect, and the city was quiet until our troops arrived the next morning.

That was actually the chief problem of the whole campaign, how to get the civil population under control while we were engaged with the Iraq army. In Ashur and Basra, looting broke out during the actual fighting; in fact, shops were being looted in the middle of the street while our forces were at one end and the police at the other firing. Some four or five days after we took over Ashur, the old city of Basra, the main bazaar was half burnt out and almost completely looted, while the police who had been left in control by us did practically nothing to stop it. The only thing that was done was by various local notables of the big families, who brought out their own private bodyguards and stood guard for various houses which they were interested to defend.

We found it almost impossible to get over to do anything after we had occupied the place. The mujtahid [religious leader] refused to take any action to control the civil population. He was still corresponding with Baghdad, and eventually went over there. We got together a local committee, composed of seven of the biggest men in the town, and asked them to form a Government, but they refused to take any responsibility. A lot might have been avoided if the Regent had sent somebody down, as he did a week later, but it was then too late. But although we had a fortnight when anything in the way of local administration was completely at a standstill, we could not do it ourselves because I and one other officer were the only two who spoke Arabic. There was not a great deal of disorder. Our chief trouble was the crowds. We put up barracks at various points, and the local populace used to assemble there until we took a prisoner once every morning and once every afternoon.

Eventually the Regent reached Baghdad and set up his new Government there. A representative was sent down to Basra, and things more or less went back to normal. The only thing was that, although the Regent was quite prepared to back us and was extremely glad of the help we had given, his ministers were not so pleased at what had turned out to be the result of their appeal for our help. When Jamil[16] first handed me a message, asking for the help of British troops, he said that he would like the loan of troops for a period of one month, which would have been ample to settle Rashid Ali as it turned out, but I do not think that he particularly liked the prospect of a British force permanently in Basra. It is interesting to note that the Armistice Commission in Syria collected two or three train loads of French arms and sent them across along the railway down to Mosul to support the Iraq rebels.

Jamil, when he came into power as Prime Minister under the Regent, had assumed no particularly energetic line of policy, and no severe action was taken against the people who had definitely supported the rebellion. There was the usual shuffle, but beyond that no further definite action was taken, and there the position remained. The feeling in the country was definitely nervous. They still then expected the Germans to produce bombs in large numbers. Although the Regent was in power, and we had troops in Basra and Baghdad, the population were nervous, and those who were definitely against us were still hoping that the Germans would bring something out of the bag and within a few months we would be out of the country once more. That situation was very much helped by our occupation of Syria in the next month, and after Syria, Iran. I think those two actions did more to restore confidence in us in the Middle East than anything else which has happened.

Some months later, I think in October, Jamil's Government fell and was replaced by one under Nuri al-Said. He went very much further than Jamil had done. His position is weaker in the country, in that he has always been considered as a British agent and he definitely had to take vigorous action in order to be able to maintain his position. He suspended a large number of the officials who had taken part against us, arrested some of the army officers, and in several ways showed the country that he was determined to deal with anybody who was working directly or indirectly on behalf of the Axis.

I do not think the vast majority of the people against us in Iraq definitely wanted the Germans in the country. They were merely using that excuse to get rid of us. But there is no doubt that a large number of them then would have helped the Germans, and I still think there is a danger, particularly at this time, of very extensive fifth column activities in Iraq.

I cannot go on with any more recent history, because shortly after this I was taken ill and had to go to Palestine, and I left the country altogether in October. *(Applause.)*

Discussion

QUESTIONER: What is the origin of the term Golden?

THE LECTURER: I could not say, but there were these four, and they gave themselves, I believe, the name of Golden Square.

Mr. HAMILTON: What about the Kurds in the north? How did they behave?

THE LECTURER: I know very little about the north myself, but when the rebellion took place, these people up there took the local government into their own hands. Eventually they compromised with the Inland Revenue in Baghdad, and the local government has been restored now.

QUESTIONER: Is it true that they were helped?

THE LECTURER: Yes, I think so. There was quite a strong German propaganda amongst the Kurds, to the effect that the Kurds were Aryans, and therefore they and the Germans [should?] get together.

SIR EDGAR BONHAM CARTER: How many troops arrived?

THE LECTURER: The first convoy was a brigade of Gurkhas, and in the later convoys were again Gurkhas, with a few British artillery and frontier forces.

THE CHAIRMAN, before closing the meeting, thanked Wing-

Commander Embling cordially on behalf of the Society and of the audience for his thrillingly interesting talk.

Notes

1 The author, Wing Commander J.R.A. Embling (1913–1959), was a university entrant from Oxford to the RAF College in 1935. He was sent to Iraq in October 1938 for language training and was subsequently Air Liaison officer in Basra. In December 1942 during World War Two he was shot down over France, but escaped with the help of the French Resistance and returned in England in March 1943. He reached the rank of Air Vice Marshal before his death in an aircraft accident in 1959.
2 King Ghazi bin Faisal, r. 1933–1939. He was educated in England, at Harrow, but did his military training at the Royal Military College, Baghdad.
3 More correctly, the Golden Square – four officers, Colonel Salah al Dink as Sabbagh, Colonel Kamal Shabib, Colonel Fahmi Said, Colonel Mahmud Salman – an anti-British group encouraged by the German ambassador in Baghdad.
4 King Faisal ibn Husayn of Iraq, r. 1921–1933.
5 The Regent was Prince 'Abd-al-llah, pro-British, killed in the 1958 coup.
6 Rashid Ali Al-Gaylani had seized power from the prime minister Nuri al-Said.
7 Taha al-Hashimi, briefly prime minister for two months from February to April 1941.
8 Left blank in original typescript.
9 Director General of Iraq State Railways.
10 Left blank in original typescript.
11 Sir Kinahan Cornwallis, British ambassador to Iraq and Royal Central Asian Society member.
12 Left blank in original text.
13 Colonel (later Lieutenant General Sir) John Glubb, better known as Glubb Pasha. British soldier who led and trained Transjordan's Arab Legion from 1939.
14 Major Axel von Blomberg, co-ordinating the German military response was not von Schier's son. He was killed on 15 May 1941 when his plane was shot down.
15 The pogrom which took place on 1–2 June 1941 was called the Farhud. The estimated death toll was between 200 and 600, with many wounded.
16 Jamil al-Midfai, prime minister between 4 June and 10 October 1941.

The Middle East
In American Opinion

By Professor H.A.R. Gibb
Lecture on 25 November 1942

Introduction

America had entered World War Two in December 1941, after its ships were bombed in Pearl Harbour by the Japanese. It declared war not only on Japan, but also on the Axis powers, Germany and Italy. American attention at the time was focussed on the conflict in Europe and the Far East, rather than the Middle East. The question of imperialism versus democracy (for example, Britain's governance of India), was an active debate. Gibb argues that European nations had a 'responsible' position in the Middle East, whereas America did not. This responsibility arose from the Treaties at the end of World War One, when the Ottoman Empire was partitioned and mandates allocated to Britain and France.

As Gibb says in this lecture, he had been studying war-time information on the Middle East that was available to the general public in America, and found it inaccurate and biased. There were historic reasons for this. Britain had been using Arab ports since the seventeenth century when its East India Company started sailing east and it had maintained diplomatic links through representatives, including a British Agent at Baghdad. Muslim pilgrims, travelling to Mecca from British India, meant there was a consular presence at Jeddah, and pacts with Persian leaders brought the region under the loose control of the Government of India. Thus there is an undercurrent in Gibb's lecture that Britain not only understood the Middle East better, having had longer experience, but resented being lectured on democracy by America.

Although Gibb described an Arab community of some 500,000 people settled in the USA, Americans did not have much personal knowledge of the Middle East. Protestant missionaries from America had travelled to Lebanon and Syria in the mid-nineteenth century and what was to become the American University of Beirut had developed from a missionary medical training college set up in 1866. American oil exploration and development started in the late 1920s and 1930s in Iraq and Saudi Arabia, but at the time of this lecture, there were few, if any academic or political institutions to study the Middle East. Gibb imagined that the new Council of Near Eastern Studies at Chicago University which was set up following the conference he attended there, would become something like the Royal Central Asian Society.

There was also the question of a Jewish homeland in Palestine, which had been proposed in the Balfour Declaration of 1917. Gibb refers in seemingly flattering tones to 'the recent book by Mr. Hanna'. This was *British Policy in Palestine* published in 1942, and the author, Paul Lamont Hanna, born in Canada, researched his book while teaching at Stanford University, USA. Hanna summed up the British dilemma towards a Jewish homeland: 'Unwilling to repudiate the Balfour Declaration, Britain was equally reluctant to enforce it fully in the face of Arab opposition.' Gibb later refers to 'a very strong, very insidious and highly concentrated Zionist propaganda' and criticises the American public for 'sentimentalism' and a 'vague sympathy . . . for oppressed people', that is, the Jews. These were by no means unfashionable views at the time.

PRIVATE AND CONFIDENTIAL
ROYAL CENTRAL ASIAN SOCIETY
Report of Meeting
held at 8 Clarges Street, London W1
on Wednesday, November 25th, 1942
Chairman: General Sir John Shea, GCB, KCMG, DSO
Professor H. A. R. Gibb lecturing[1]

THE CHAIRMAN: Ladies and Gentlemen, Mr. H. A. R. Gibb, who has kindly consented to come and talk to us to-day, is an Arabic scholar of note and distinction, not only in the Near and Middle East but also in this country and in America. He has lately been in America, and he will tell you of the American reactions to the Middle Eastern question. (*Applause.*)

In these days, when a ten days' visit to the capitals of a number of countries is sufficient to make one an authority on the political problems of that region, I suppose ten weeks in America is quite enough to qualify me as an expert on every conceivable subject relating to America. But I do not imagine that the Royal Central Asian Society has taken that as the reason for asking me to speak here to-day. My qualifications for accepting this invitation are two: that for three years and more I have seen the great majority of the reports sent by American Correspondents in the Middle East to their newspapers in all parts of America, and that cuttings from the main American news-papers have passed through my hands, so that I have been able to form in that way a certain general judgment as to the value of these news-paper reports; and, secondly, that I went over at the invitation of the University of Chicago, the Harris Foundation of the University of Chicago,[2] to a conference held at Chicago dealing with questions affecting the Near East, at which practically all the American author-ities on Near Eastern subjects were present. By authorities I mean, first of all, the academic writers and students, a certain number of officials and practical business men, and also representatives of various polit-ical committees, and for a week we were engaged in a fairly general discussion on all kinds of topics of the present day. I suppose this was a unique opportunity of attempting to assess the opinions which are held by the informed sections of Americans on questions affecting the Middle East.

Before I go on, may I apparently digress for a little. One of the things which I have learned in the last three years – learned in a way which has made it actual to me – is the enormous difference between the various types of information. There is, first of all, the long range, what one may perhaps call academic information, information which is based upon a long view of historical developments, which pays most attention to the slow cumulative movements that are taking place in different parts of the world, and which is perhaps a little impatient of the surface movements which agitate political life and international relations from time to time.

On the other hand, there is that other kind of information, which is concerned chiefly with those surface movements and political agita-tions, the day to day political information, and here too there are two different kinds. There is the information about day to day events which is strictly accurate, informed not only of what goes on on the surface but what goes on underneath the surface, the kind of information which represents the best official information, and which, of course, is rarely if ever accessible to the general public. In the second place, there is the public information on these day to day happenings which is conveyed chiefly by means of newspaper correspondents, and in the same way concentrates itself entirely upon local events but sometimes tries more or less to relate them to their background.

The difference or the likeness between what I have called the day to day private information and the day to day public information is the test of good journalism. If the public information is good, it does not greatly differ in regard to the essential features from the official information, even if the details are jealously preserved as a secret in official circles, so that on the whole the public has a pretty good idea of what is going on. In trying to keep the level of public information relatively close to the official information, there lies the first difficulty for the outsider, the first responsibility which rests upon the publicist. But there is a second difficulty, and that is the difficulty of combining what I have called the academic information with the day to day political information; and that difficulty is one which is not felt exclusively by the publicist. It is felt, of course, by the publicist; by that I mean the man who is primarily interested in the day to day business and is not an academic student. But it is also felt in official circles.

If I may perhaps develop a metaphor a little at some length, the two kinds of information I have been dealing with are like the two views that you can take about the movement of the sea: the long term corresponds to the slow, gradual movement of the tides; the short-term corresponds to the rather choppy but much more obvious movement of the waves.

I suppose that it is only since in the last three years or so I have been associated with work which is done in official circles,[3] that I have come to realize how it is that many Governments, not excluding H.M. Government on occasions, have been so occupied in watching the movement of the waves that they have suddenly found themselves cut off by the rising tide and have had to make a somewhat undignified scramble back to dry land. One may pursue the metaphor a little further, and say that sometimes, watching it through a telescope, they have found themselves left high and dry as the tide has receded. At all events, the point I do want to make clear is that it is almost as difficult to combine the official information with long-term study, as it is to combine the more popular journalistic information with long-term study.

So far as this country is concerned, those gaps between the academic and day to day information, and between official and public day to day information are on the whole fairly well closed, and they are closed because there have been so many official and private contacts with different parts of the Near East and between those who are concerned with different problems of the Near East. The gap exists, and I suppose it always will to a certain extent exist, but nevertheless I think we may say that all who are genuinely interested in Near Eastern problems in this country are able on the whole to get a fairly clear and accurate picture even without being officials as to both the long- term and the short-term information.

In the United States it is not so. The gap between the two different kinds of information, and also between the short and long-term information is very much wider. There is a large number of serious students of long-term developments in the United States, possibly larger than there is in Great Britain. There is a very large number of very estimable long-term studies published in the United States by American scholars, but, on the other hand, in so far as the, day to day information is concerned, the general mass are extremely badly informed, and the responsibility for that rests, it seems to me, upon the recklessness of newspaper reports in the United States.

I said at the beginning that for three years I had been studying cuttings from all the most important newspapers in the United States by correspondents, temporary or permanent correspondents, in the Middle East. One derives a certain sardonic amusement out of them, but it is a rather sobering reflection that there are scarcely any of those reports, even when they are written by men of outstanding eminence in their profession, which do not contain either one or more very serious mis-statements of fact or serious misinterpretations of the situation.

If I may mention one of the most eminent of American journalists, Harry Emery Barnes, was sent out on a mission, by the New York Times, I think, the mission on which he eventually met his death in Jugoslavia. He published three extremely interesting articles, but it was quite obvious to anyone who really knew the situation in Egypt and Iraq that those articles represented the view of a certain group of persons and did not represent at all the facts of the situation. Throughout there was a given bias, which was due to the fact that the writer had made a very genuine effort to try and arrive at the real facts of the situation, but because of his lack of background information, because of his lack of ability to judge the quality of his informers, inevitably the picture he presented was a one-sided picture.

I do not want to mention names; it is perhaps rather invidious, but the fact remains that it is extremely difficult for the average American citizen to obtain a clear and reasonably accurate statement of facts relating to Middle Eastern countries. I am not speaking here of pure propagandists. From them one neither expects nor does one, of course, ever get clear and accurate statements.

American academic study, on the contrary, the long-term study done by American experts, is quite different. That is distinguished by technical skill and by immense patience and perseverance in the pursuit of the elusive truth. Many, many names will occur to you here – such names as Earle on Turkey,[4] Philip Ireland on Iraq,[5] and some of you have already seen Paul Hanna's book on Palestine.[6] All of these are serious, worth-while studies which can be read with profit not only in America but also in this country. But from our point of view they suffer from three deficiencies, two of which at least can be excused.

The first is that they have no access to British official information. I do not think it can be too strongly emphasized that, for the greater part of the Middle East, there is only one source which gives absolutely accurate information, and that is British official papers. No other official papers can give it, because no other embassies, or consulates, do know in fact what has happened in certain circumstances. For that, of course, one must except to a certain extent Syria and Lebanon, where only the French official papers can give absolutely detailed accurate information. Neither has the British public got access to official papers, but because of the constant intercourse which goes on between those who are concerned and interested in and related to the Near East, the amount of information available to the British public is on the whole accurate in its general lines, which is, I think, a very important thing.

Incidentally, I should like to say that it is a tremendous pity that British official papers are held up so long before publication. I think the limit is still fifty years before they can be published. Many official papers of even a hundred years ago have not been published, but as I am speaking in a confidential group here, let me take one example.

Like most people I shared a certain view as to British policy in Persia since the last war, and it is only since I have been able to read the British official papers concerning policy since that I have realized how extraordinarily wrong my view was and the view that is held by the general public on the internal and international history of Persia in the last twenty years. That is one obvious weakness, that accuracy on detailed matters of fact is not always possible for those writers.

The second is – and this is a rather more general problem – a certain characteristic of technique, which is to neglect personal elements. That is something which is characteristic of technique all over the world. Technical methods tend to reduce things to categories, to sort them all out, label them, and then by using the recognized processes you jumble them up and eventually something comes out and your problem is solved. That is the essence of technique.

Let us remember that technical development in the United States has gone a tremendous deal further than in this country. Technical methods have entered very much more – here I speak subject to correction – into American life than into our lives. When the British Government wants a ship built, it says to British shipbuilders, "How soon can you build me a ship?" and the builder says, "In six, or eight, or twelve months." The American Government puts the question, and Mr Kaiser says, "In four days," and produces the ship in four days.[7] The one is using all the resources of technique, whereas the other is thinking still in terms that are a little personal, thinking of what workmen will do instead of what machines will do.

The same idea underlies Mr. Wendell Willkie's[8] recent demand that all Colonial problems should be settled under a time schedule, that is, everything can be fitted in to just such and such a system of nicely labelled compartments. There is a great deal of merit in that. It is a thing we have not got enough of. But it means, first of all, a tendency to underrate the personal elements which enter into political problems all over the world, and especially into the political life and problems of the Near and Middle East.

That element of lack of realization of the personal element is strengthened by the fact that very few of the writers do in fact know the personalities, or have had personal touch with the people or events they are writing about, that they are aware sometimes of the social forces, but they are not aware of the relative weight of the persons who are playing a part in those social forces. That does not only produce a certain lack of real body in what they write, but also produces another serious defect from the purely technical point of view, that they cannot appreciate the relative value of the authorities they are quoting.

If I may take an example from the recent book by Mr. Hanna, which I think an excellent bit of work. There is in one place a statement made by him, which would be a statement of crucial importance; but when you look up his reference, you find it is to an article written by an extreme Zionist in the *Manchester Guardian*. Every British writer would know at once what reliance to place upon that particular writer's articles in that particular place: but it is that lack of the personal knowledge which is bound to a certain extent to limit the thoroughness and effectiveness of these writers.

There is a third characteristic of most American work dealing with the Middle East, and that is that it presents predominantly what I may call an A.U.B. point of view, i.e. it is influenced by the views and ideas of the American University of Beirut. That is an institution on which better qualified people here than I can express a judgment. I have a very, very high respect for it, and very happy memories of my stays there and contacts. But one result of the A.U.B. point of view is this, that it over-values the Syrian and Lebanese attitude. It places Syria and Lebanon too much in the foreground and gives too much weight to their point of view in the general analysis of Near Eastern problems.

As a result of the political developments of the last twenty years, the Syrian point of view is slightly eccentric. That is, it is governed too much by the reaction towards the problem of relations with France, and is so much concentrated on that as not to be able to take in the general problems with the same freedom which one would find even in Iraq, although that too suffers from something of the same weakness or the same concentration.

I have gone at great length into these weaknesses, but let me repeat again that there is an enormous amount of very valuable work which has been done by American scholars on these questions, and that in the grasp of essentials there is very little to criticize, and very much to take to heart. But, as I have suggested, there is an enormous gap between the work of these informed observers and the mass of the American public.

There seems to me to be a considerable amount of what one can only call sentimentalism, which finds expression in such things as vague sympathy for any group of persons who can be called an oppressed people. It is very easy at any time to put forward a certain amount of information or evidence, corresponding to these rather sentimental ideas about oppression which are held in a great many circles, who are exposed at the same time to a very strong, very insidious and highly concentrated Zionist propaganda. These necessarily to a great extent affect and distort the thinking of the American public as a whole on Middle Eastern questions, so that the problem of future American views and opinions about the Middle East must depend very largely upon the extent to which the considered educated opinion is able to counter and to educate the popular public opinion.

I believe that it is possible that it may do so, and it was very largely because of the interest of this problem that I appreciate the enormous advantage which it was to me to be able to take part in that conference which was held at Chicago, which did represent American educated opinion on the Middle East at its best.

I want to finish off by saying a very little about that conference. I cannot say a great deal because as a conference it took no votes and passed no resolutions, and its proceedings were strictly confidential. I can only give rather general impressions. It seemed to me quite clear that the general atmosphere of that conference, when it first met, was one of confident knowledge of and ability to handle the problems which it was going to deal with. But at the same time there was something which it shared to a certain extent with what I have called sentimental public opinion.

One was a suspicion of British policy. The second was that doctrine of freedom which was considered rather as a pendent to condemnation of so-called exploitation. Those two ideas were – I think it is not unfair to say – pretty obviously in evidence in a great deal of the discussions which went on at the conference. But there was along with that – and this is a very striking feature – much evidence of extreme openness of mind, a readiness to listen to and weigh evidence and opinions, and to make up afresh one's mind on questions which perhaps one thought one had already made up one's mind on. As the conference went on, it is quite clear that that process was taking place in a very large measure throughout the conference as a whole.

To start with there was a certain suspicion of British policy, a certain readiness to assume that all that is necessary is to clear out and freedom will result – I mean for example clear out of Iraq, and Iraq would be free. The same with Saudi Arabia. A suggestion that because Turkey is an independent, self-governing State, there is therefore no problem about Turkey at all. Here again we come back to this technical way of looking at things. Turkey has been solved, and for that reason it stands out. There is nothing further to be done about it. Whereas Egypt, Iraq, Palestine, Syria, Arabia – these have not been solved, and a solution has to be found, and the first step towards that solution is, "Leave them alone."

There were several things which contributed a little towards shaking that opinion. One arose out of the fact that leaving them alone has been associated in the popular mind with the suggestion that there is a steady process of what one may call social progress in all Middle Eastern countries.

It fell to me to speak at one of the public meetings of the Institute on this question of social progress in the Middle East, and without my actually knowing in advance how the argument was going to work out, it did in fact, as it worked itself out, lead to something like a denial that there was such a thing as social progress in the Middle East, in the sense that the social ideals toward which the Middle Eastern countries are working are not the social ideals of Western Europe, or of the United States, and to the realisation that the more the Eastern countries develop their own freedom, the more they will diverge from Western European or American ideas of social development; this naturally went counter to the idea that the Middle East was naturally progressing in a certain direction, and all that was necessary to complete that progress was to allow each country to live upon its own without any kind of external interference or pressure.

The second, and much more effective thing came when the question of Palestine came up for discussion. It was then most patent to the most unwilling member of the conference that the problem of Palestine was above all a personal problem. The conference very wisely had included a certain number of persons of Arab origin in its numbers and persons of Jewish origin and faith, and the personal element at that meeting forced itself on everybody's notice, and there was no getting away from it. That was another step in the direction of what I might call the gradual change over of view.

But, even so, there was still a third step which had to come, and it was reached only rather unwillingly, rather as a result of the logical development of the argument as it proceeded day after day. That was the result of the fact that, as I have said, the A.U.B. attitude was very much in the foreground, and it tended to focus on the difference between the position which America holds in the Near East and the position held by the European nations. What is this due to? At first, the general answer would have been, "This is due to the fact that the Americans are not Imperialist and the European nations are." But gradually it was driven home, as the conference proceeded, that the explanation was not so simple as Imperialism versus non-Imperialism. It was more that the European nations have been responsible, and the Americans have had no responsiblity.

Then came, of course, this very awkward question, which had to be faced, "Is the United States justified in enjoying privilege without responsibility?" as undoubtedly it has done in Syria. And, secondly, can it go on taking advantage of passing responsibility on to others, not so much in Syria as in the Persian Gulf where it is an economic question, where American interests are definitely and irretrievably engaged.

So, as I say, rather unwillingly, with a certain amount of rather sharp opposition from certain members of the conference, there was quite a perceptible movement of feeling that after all the United States had a certain duty to perform as well as a certain ideal to uphold; and that that duty involved doing certain things which were rather distasteful. It involved, for example, taking a hand in trying to solve questions in the Middle East. Above all, it involved taking a hand in bearing some of the burden of maintaining order in the Middle East, realizing that it was not just so easy. For instance, what would happen to all those precious oil deposits in the Persian Gulf if Great Britain and Russia and all the European States were simply to withdraw? How could there possibly be, not merely a guarantee for American interests, because do not let it be imagined that they were thinking solely in terms of American interests, but also in terms of world interests? After all, this Persian Gulf area is going to be one of the great centres of supply for the whole world. They were thinking in terms of world organization, but with the realization that the United States has to take its place in guaranteeing the working of the world system which is going to preserve stability in the Middle East.

The problem remains, of course, how far is educated opinion in the United States going to be able to impress itself sufficiently upon a mass of uneducated opinion to get that more generally realised?

There are very few of us here who would not welcome the development of American opinion in the direction of taking part in maintaining the controls which are going to maintain stability and security in the Middle East. There are very few of us who would not accept the fact that an American participation in those controls would bring a greater breadth of vision into the organizations with which the Middle East is at present concerned.

But there does remain a point which one cannot help being uneasy about, that the Middle East is likely to be always one of the awkward problems after the war; and it is an area in which very small differences of opinion and very small differences of view may have very serious consequences. We have not solved the problem if it is only settled that after all America is going to come in and play her part in preserving world order and world security in the Middle East. We have only, as it were, begun to lay the foundations of an order which is going to present its own problems, and there again it seems to me that we shall never be able adequately to keep in step unless instructed American opinion is able to maintain itself on top of popular uninstructed opinion. How that is to be done, is a question which I am rather thankful that I have not got to try and answer here. *(Applause.)*

Discussion

MRS PATRICK NESS: What function is performed by the British Bureau of Information in the States under Professor Winifred Cullis in giving adequate information?

PROF. GIBB: The British Institute does nothing in the way of propaganda. It only supplies information asked for.

A MEMBER: You say they are at last beginning in America to realize that this word Imperialism does mean responsibility and is not necessarily entirely selfish but very altruistic as well. The sooner America appreciates that point, the sooner she will understand our problems, not only in the Near East but everywhere else. It is essential that that should be done, and that America should realize what Imperialism means.

We have kept the peace for a hundred years by our fleet. As far as the Near East is concerned, it is the Clapham Junction of the Far East.

The United States do not understand how much our Navy has done for world peace by taking charge. How can this Society, or how can we either individually or as a Society help to put it across to the Americans one way or another what Imperialism really means, particularly with regard to the Near East, but even generally?

PROF. GIBB: I do not know that I can answer that question. I think journalism is doing a great deal already.

A MEMBER: I think so too, but let us increase it.

PROF. GIBB: One of the results of the Chicago conference was that the conference constituted itself a Council of Near Eastern Studies, which is already therefore in existence. In fact, I have paid my $1 for membership subscription. Ultimately it is intended to create a body something like the R.C.A.S. [Royal Central Asian Society] to study Near Eastern questions in the U.S.A., and I presume that this Society will be in fairly close touch with it.

SIR PERCY SYKES: I hear from an American banker, a very well-informed man, a member of the R.C.A.S., every two months or so, when he gives me the American opinion on all these questions. He points out that the intenseness of the actual situation, as viewed from people living in the country, is lacking because missionaries, with the best intentions in the world, are always bringing in the narrowed line.

I have studied the Americans very closely, and I have come to the conclusion that they are what I call shop-window dressers. They want to pick up just enough information to be able to talk about the subject at a dinner party, and they never go beyond. There was never any real knowledge of the Middle East. They were very good to me and very nice, but Prof. Jackson of Columbia University, who is a member of this Society and stayed with me in Persia, was the only American I met who could talk about any of these subjects. They got hold of something that makes a good story and put it down, and then they all rang the changes on our Imperialism, as they say, which means responsibility. That will have to be changed, if they are going to help.

A MEMBER: I feel, Sir, that this war has forced our American friends into tackling problems in these countries which they perhaps did not realize before, at any rate did not realize how difficult they were.

I should like to call the attention of the Society to three names. The late Mr. Knabenshue, American Consul-General in Baghdad who was one of the best friends Britain ever had. Both in Baluchistan, and previously in Syria, and lastly in Baghdad, though our stock was very low, Mr Knabenshue did what nobody else could have done perhaps, he helped the British Empire to pull through a very difficult time, and did all he could for us and showed that friendship which perhaps no other nation in the world could show except America in our time of stress.

The second name is that of an American diplomat also, i.e. Mr. Wadsworth, who has recently been appointed to Beirut. He has now been appointed to Syria, to represent them as their diplomatic agent in Lebanon and Syria. I cannot imagine from my knowledge of American diplomats anyone more suited than Mr. George Wadsworth, and he has already received a warm welcome from our diplomats there.

The third is Bayard Dodge, the President of the American University of Beirut. Whatever the weaknesses of the A.U.B. – there are weaknesses no doubt, but there are many strengths, and the strengths lie in Bayard Dodge, his personality and character. I regard him as one of the great men at present living in that part of the world. He would be of immense value to us and to the Americans and to other European nations in building up the Middle East after the war.

Those three names are enough to prove that America is not behindhand altogether in seeing what the difficulties are and in helping us to face them. *(Applause.)*

A MEMBER: Mr. Gibb referred with appreciation to the academic student type of information with regard to international affairs, and he gave some instances, e.g. the work of Philip Ireland and Earle. To what extent can we regard the academic student class as guides in current events? I ask the question because Mr. Gibb emphasized the point that official information on events is so long delayed in publication that it seems to me that these students have nothing except past history and current administrational reports on events to go on, which, though no doubt always accurate are never very informative. Anybody who merely repeated what he had seen in the usual official report might be completely misled. Should we regard those students merely as of historian significance, or as competent and helpful guides to giving that information to the American public and guiding current opinion on public events?

PROF. GIBB: There are two different kinds of student. There are those who are purely interested in the tracing out of an historical problem, or some technical problem, and there they have a certain value.

There is the second kind of academic student, who does seriously attempt to get the background for current affairs. The value of that type is that such students do provide a solid background, without which any kind of appreciation of current events is quite impossible. It is pretty obvious that academic students can never of themselves really supply the need for day to day information. But what they can do is to create a body of knowledge which is at the disposal of the persons who, firstly, purvey, and, secondly, those who consume the day to day information. It is that gap which has been to a considerable extent closed in Great Britain, which is not yet closed in the U.S.A., and which if any enlightened public opinion is to be created in the U.S.A. must be closed

A MEMBER (lady): Might it not be said now that, instead of French, English is the lingua franca of the Near East? There is the Robert College, the College at Beirut, and all the Assyrians[9] who have had a European education. Is it not a drawback that, although the language is English, the dissemination of that English language is American. All these people look to America as their sort of spiritual home and not to Britain, and we have no central place where we can disseminate British ideas.

On the subject of working together, I wonder if it has ever been taken into consideration that in the Oil Company – my husband was in charge of the oil survey – the British, French, American and Dutch all work together in complete amity. If something like that could be done on a larger scale, it would be of great benefit. Could not this Society do something to open up contacts in that way?

PROF. GIBB: I cannot answer the second part of your question, but as for the first, were you referring particularly to Syria or Iraq?

A MEMBER: The whole of the Near East.

PROF. GIBB: That is not true certainly of Egypt. I should not say that it was necessarily true of Palestine. It certainly is the case in Syria and Lebanon, because the American University of Beirut has a very fine tradition, which we should not ever attempt to do anything to counteract. I have not enough personal knowledge of Iraq to be able to confirm or reject your statement, but I think it is very likely, because after all most students in Iraq who do have a University education do go to the American University at Beirut.

A MEMBER: The British Council are practically taking charge of that problem, I think, and therefore we are relieved of it.

A MEMBER: There is in the United States a community of about half a million of Arabs with a Press of their own. I wondered how far that affects the trend of American opinion?

PROF. GIBB: I should have said something about that problem. One of my ideas, when I went over to the United States, was that I should see as much as possible of the Arab community. But I changed my mind fairly soon after seeing a representative selection chiefly in the Middle West. I went to a conference and had a good deal of conversation with their leading members, and what I have to say is based very largely upon the experience there and the experience of meeting a certain number of these Syrian Arabs.

The Syrian Arab community consists really of two groups: those who emigrated from Syria and those who are American-born. The

American-born by now must be two-thirds of the whole community. The Syrian-born community is still interested in Syrian politics, but it is divided amongst itself. Some of them are Pan-Syrians or Pan-Arabs, and some of them are Lebanese Nationalists. Incidentally at Detroit, where there is a large Moslem as well as a large Lebanite community, the two do not mix at all.

The American-born Syrians are very much more remote from Near Eastern politics. A certain number of them, through family influences, do take a certain interest in Syria. Very, very few of them take enough interest to be able to read even a little Arabic. The great majority of the American-born Syrians are completely uninterested in Syrian politics: They say, and it seems to me very rightly after all, "We are Americans. We do not really care what those people over there are doing, whether they are Syrians or Lebanese, or whether they fight one another, or what they do."

That is the attitude. It is a little deplored by their fathers and mothers and grandparents, but it is very natural and means in effect, even if the Syrians were prepared to take any kind of active part, they would not be able to take a united part, that those who were interested would be divided amongst themselves; and the great majority are not interested at all.

But the question really does not arise as to what attitude they would take because they don't. There is really no effective Syrian-Arab movement in the sense of trying to explain to Americans what are the realities of the Middle Eastern situation outside the very small group which are centred round Prof. Hitti[10] at Princeton University. He is the spokesman and makes a certain amount of stir.

Partly also the Syrians do not want to be mixed up, I think in problems of American policy in the Near East; they do not want to be considered Semites, and are afraid of being implicated in the anti-Semitic feeling.

THE CHAIRMAN: Ladies and Gentlemen, Mr. Gibb has given us such an erudite and interesting exposition of his subject, that I am certain we could go on asking him questions for the best part of the afternoon. But we have found it convenient always to put a time limit on these lectures, and our time is up.

I am sure I am voicing your opinion when I tell him how very deeply grateful we are to him for having come and talked to us this afternoon. *(Applause.)*

Notes

1 Professor (later Sir) Hamilton Alexander Rosskeen Gibb (1895–1971) was born in Alexandria and schooled in Scotland. He studied Arabic at

the School of Oriental Studies (later SOAS) and taught there after gradu-
ating, before moving to St John's College Oxford in 1937 where he taught
for thirteen years. He became Visiting Professor at Harvard University in
1950 and full time professor of Arabic there in 1955. Later, he became
Director of Harvard Center For Middle Eastern Studies.

2 The Norman Wait Harris Foundation was the sponsoring body for the
conference on 'The Near East: Problems and Prospects' that was held at
the University of Chicago from 25–30 June 1942. Professor Gibb delivered two lectures: 'Social Change in the Near East' and 'The Future for
Arab Unity'. Information from Daniel Meyer, Archivist at the University
of Chicago Library, Illinois.

3 Gibb worked in the Research Department of the Foreign Office during
the war.

4 Dr Edward Mead Earle wrote *Turkey, The Great Powers, and the
Baghdad Railway, a Study in Imperialism* published in 1924. He was one
time Assistant Professor of History at Columbia University.

5 Philip Ireland published *Iraq: a study in Political Development* in 1938.

6 *British Policy in Palestine* by Paul Hanna was published in 1942.

7 Henry Kaiser was an American industrialist. Early in November 1942 he
built a 10,500 cargo ship in four days at the Kaiser Shipyard in California.

8 Wendell Willkie was an American lawyer who stood against President
Roosevelt in the 1940 election and subsequently became an 'ambassador
at large', opposing imperialism and colonialism.

9 Assyrian was used interchangeably with Syrian at this period.

10 Professor Philip Hitti was educated at the American University of Beirut
and later taught semitic and oriental languages at Columbia and Princeton
Universities in the United States. He was opposed to the creation of Israel.

Post-war Britain and the Middle East

By Lt. Colonel S.H. Slater, Indian Army
Lecture on 20 January 1943

Introduction

Following the sudden death of King Ghazi bin Faisal of Iraq in 1939, the country was being governed by the prince-regent 'Abd al-llah during the minority of his nephew, the future king. The regency saw a succession of army coups d'etat that had brought Rashid Ali to power for a brief period as prime minister and the British defence of the Royal Air Force base at Habbaniya (see the first lecture 'Iraq 1942'). Subsequently 'Abd al-llah allied Iraq with the Allies against the Axis Powers of Germany, Italy and Japan.

The lecturer summarises the short history of Iraq from the formal abolition of the Ottoman Empire in 1922 to a 'semblance' of independence ten years later and its admission to the League of Nations. Although Slater himself had been part of this process until 1924, he thought the rush to self-government was over-confident and unwise. After the death of Faisal I, the first British-appointed king of Iraq in 1933, there were tribal uprisings, and a massacre of Assyrians in the north of the country.

In the space of twenty years, Britain had turned the new country, with its 'strong personality', a taste for material prosperity, and a feeling of friendship towards the British, into an unstable state, with an expensive government which had no real public support. Tribal and urban rivalry was stronger now than it had been under the Ottoman thumb, and a former friendship for the British 'grievously impaired'. It is a condemnation of British policy.

Slater forecast that after the war an international body would be responsible for securing world peace and small countries like Iraq would have to comply. There would be no room for the Iraqi army.

Britain should work with Iraq developing its natural resources and improving irrigation, agriculture and communications. He felt this was the only way to make amends for 'separating Iraq from her historic connections' and putting her in a false position of isolation.

The discussion after the lecture is revealing. Several speakers presciently warned of the danger of a strong, and at times, out of control army in Iraq that had started meddling in politics. The 'Palestine question' was aired again, but more interesting is the mention of the Kurds as 'troublesome people'. Kurds had risen against the British in Iraq, and were subjected to bombing raids by the RAF in the 1920s and 30s.

The Central Asian Society had advocated a School of Oriental Studies in London before the first world war. The Chairman for this lecture, Mr H. de Burgh Codrington, criticises the School (now the School of Oriental & African Studies), for its lack of training.

PRIVATE AND CONFIDENTIAL
ROYAL CENTRAL ASIAN SOCIETY
Report of a Meeting
held at 8 Clarges Street, London W1
on Wednesday, January 20th, 1943, at 1.30 p.m.
Chairman: Mr. H. De B. Codrington
Mr. S. H. Slater, CMG. CIE lecturing[1]

I see I am down to open a discussion on "Post War Britain and the Middle East." I cannot possibly do all that in twenty minutes, and so, if you do not mind, I will confine myself mainly to Iraq. I should think we would all agree that the Middle East is not a single entity, political or economic entity, but is composed of a large number of very diverse units, of which one is Iraq.

There is one other small point of explanation, and that is that the period to which my remarks will apply is up to about the middle of 1941.

Iraq has lately been again in the news, and I am sure that everyone here will welcome the recent announcement that Iraq is now actively allied with the United Nations [the Allies] against the Axis Powers. *(Applause.)* What the exact significance of that is, or what its bearing should be on what I am going to say, I cannot tell. I cannot attempt to forecast that now, but very likely that is a point which may be raised in the subsequent discussion.

I have for a long time been among the critics of our policy since 1920 in the Middle East, and particularly in Iraq; but I would not waste time talking about it now, if it were not for my belief that the end of the war will bring a great opportunity for revising that policy. No one can say what changes are likely to take place, but I may perhaps suggest one or two probabilities. One is that Great Britain will not be in a position, even if it desired, to pursue a separate or exclusive policy in the Middle East: and another is that the great preoccupation of the Allied Powers after the war will be the setting up of some international system or scheme of defence, and that the main object will be, not so much the protection or the safeguarding of particular interests as the peace of the world.

So I think I may say that our Imperial Interests will no longer require that we should maintain a predominant position in the Middle East. That is perhaps rather a challenging statement to make. I have not in mind any diminution in Imperial interest, but rather a change of direction.

Perhaps I can best illustrate my meaning if you will allow me to give a very slight account of how it was that we came to establish our position in the Middle East. It is an interesting episode in a very famous chapter of British history. We had to consider the protection of India. Throughout the nineteenth century there was general manoeuvring on the part of European Powers for routes to the East. For a long time during the Napoleonic era, France was our declared competitor in and beyond the Mediterranean, and so long as Egypt seemed to be under French influence, our efforts were directed to securing access to the Persian Gulf by the overland route. Later, those efforts were illustrated by many well-known enterprises, mostly connected with the name of Chesney,[2] for convenient routes across the desert. These enterprises were dropped when, later, we secured transit rights across the Egyptian delta and eventually the control of the Suez Canal; and attention was then for a time diverted from the Middle East.

Then came Russia, and that seemed to be a more proximate peril because of the possibility of movement through Persia down to the Persian Gulf, and the establishment of outposts and bases on the Persian Gulf. That menace seemed at the time so threatening that it led to a warning, delivered by the then Foreign Secretary, Lord Lansdowne, in 1883, to the effect that the British Government would regard the establishment of any such bases or posts as a menace to British interests, which it would oppose by all the means in its power.

Our attention was thus drawn back again to the Middle East, and, to counter these menaces, steps were continued to establish representatives in Basra and Baghdad, and the scope of the Government of India was gradually extended over the Persian Gulf by a series of measures, which culminated in a general compact with the Sheikhs in that region. Lord Curzon, in a speech which he made at that time to the assembled Sheikhs, and through them to the world at large, declared the policy of the Government. "The great Empire of India," he said, "which it is our duty to defend, lies almost at your gates. The peace of these waters must still be maintained. Your independence will be upheld, and the influence of the British Government must remain supreme."[3] That is the authentic note of the confident imperialism of those men and those times.

Lastly came the menace (more substantial perhaps) from Germany, and this led to an estrangement with Turkey, which was unfortunate, because it had been our traditional policy to be good friends with Turkey, and the maintenance of the integrity of the Ottoman Empire had always been a cardinal feature of British policy. But Turkey appeared then as the head of the Islamic world, and in that capacity she was much sought after by European Powers, who were anxious to undermine British influence in the East.

That is a very hasty sketch of the way in which our Imperial interests came to be connected with the Persian Gulf.

Now the picture has changed. It has changed greatly. Those dangers which menaced us in those days are no longer there. They will at any rate have receded far into the background, and there will be room for a new policy. The keynote of the new Imperial policy, as I see it, will be not so much to secure strategic points, as to encourage the full development and production of the natural resources of the British Empire for the common good of mankind.

That is what I mean by saying there will be an opportunity for revision. But why should the policy be revised? To answer that question, I must very briefly recount how that policy began, what shape it took, and what has come of it.

The war of 1914–1918 seemed to offer a great opportunity for completing our imperial policy, the former policy that I have just been describing. What had formerly been a sphere of influence had now become a conquered territory, disposable, in theory at any rate, at the will of the conquerors. Naturally the solution which suggested itself to men's minds at that time, Arab as well as British, was the establishment of a direct British control in that region.

But then there occurred an event, or a series of events, which (to quote a significant phrase used by Gertrude Bell[4] at the time) "gave a new turn to the native mind" – and, she might have added, to the British mind also. President Wilson's Fourteen Points, and the Anglo-French Declaration which was published in November 1918, awakened men's minds to the ideas of nationalism, of self-determination, ideas which had already been vigorously canvassed on the

Western side of the desert as the culmination of the Arab revolt against the Turks and their participation with us in the conquest of Palestine and Syria.

Simultaneously, the need for financial economy, the arrangements that we had entered into with the French in Syria, and certain pressure by our American Allies, made it difficult for us, if not impossible, at that time to contemplate the setting up of a direct British administration; and these considerations were reinforced by the Arab rising of 1920.

The alternative policy of departure or evacuation was contrary to every consideration of policy then prevailing – the protection of the route to India, the value of Iraq as a source of oil supply and air communications, and also our obligations of honour to a people whom we had recently separated from their Turkish rulers. That was a very tangled and complex situation, resulting in a rather hybrid policy.

Eventually the doctrinaire ideas of nationalism and self-determination prevailed – ideas gilded by romantic visions of the revival of the glories of the Abbasid era, and strengthened by the undoubted merits of the Shereefian candidate for the throne.[5]

We set up in 1921 an Arab Government in Iraq in the form of a constitutional monarchy, vested in the Shereefian family with a Parliament and a Ministry formed as far as possible on the British model.

Throughout the mandate period, that is until 1932, the responsibility for administration remained with the British Government and the British High Commissioner. The term "mandate" being distasteful to national sentiment, the relations between the two Governments were from a very early date expressed in the form of a treaty, but the mandate in theory remained.

In 1932 the mandate was formally terminated, Iraq was admitted to the League under the sponsorship of Great Britain, and a new treaty was concluded. That was certainly a very astonishing achievement – to have taken what had been a backward province of the Ottoman Empire, and to convert it in the space of a very few years into the semblance at any rate of an independent State, administering its own laws, and taking a large share of responsibility for its defence. That was indeed an achievement.

How was it that so difficult and formidable a task was so rapidly accomplished? Much must be attributed to the genius of those who were behind that policy at the time, the inspiration of T. E. Lawrence, the diplomatic skill of Sir Percy Cox[6] and the talent and enthusiasm of Gertrude Bell, to pick out only three of the most conspicuous names.

But the real reason has far-reaching implications: it was simply that speed was essential to the policy which the British Government deemed most suited to meet the various local and international exigencies of the moment. In other words, it was not the intrinsic merits of Iraq's claim to independence so much as the pressure of external factors that determined the speed of the operation. On the merits there were many differences of opinion. Opposition was very strong, both on the British and the Iraqi side. Iraqi opposition came partly from those extreme Nationalists who wanted a very much fuller form of self-government, partly from some rival candidates for the throne, and partly from a section which definitely distrusted nationalist ambition and which preferred British control.

British opposition was also varied. It came partly from the advocates of evacuation – "the lock-stock-and-barrel" people; partly from the antiquarian-minded, who were in favour of old-style colonizing policy; but a great deal of it came from a very strong body of opinion, which felt that Iraq had no real qualifications for self-government at that time, and that the wisest course was the retention of British control, with a wide and liberal admixture of Arabs in the administration. The protagonist of that school of thought was the late Sir Arnold Wilson.[7]

As I have said, the other idea, the independent State plan, prevailed, and though very considerable provision was made at the outset for British supervision and control, it was not long before the bluff was called, and, step by step, the Arab façade permeated the entire structure.

May I recapitulate the motives of our policy? We certainly were strongly influenced by the idea of self-determination. We had, under stress of war, made various promises to the Arabs generally and to the Hedjaz ruling house in particular.[8] We could not well do in Iraq what we should not like the French to do in Syria. We had important material interests. We thought it necessary to retain paramount influence on the route to India, and finally we could not afford direct occupation, or we thought we could not.

There you have a very complex assortment of motives, some of them obviously inconsistent with others, Arab nationalism and self-determination seem to have been the predominant ideas. But how could they be really said to apply to Iraq? There was no traditional unity between the inhabitants of Iraq and those of the rest of Arabia. There had never been an Iraqi nation. Iraq had had no active share in the rising against the Turks. The promise of an independent Arab State had been made to the ruler of the Hedjaz, not to the Arabs of Iraq who had no part or lot in his struggle.

It strikes me that that was a very curious idea of self-determination. It was perhaps typical of the times that it was exploited with astonishing and almost aggressive enthusiasm. Personal liking of British for Arab is, of course, traditional, and it had recently received a great impetus in the new fellow-ship which Lawrence had created with the Arabs in the Hedjaz. Such personalities as the late Jafar Pasha,[9] his brother-in-law the present Prime Minister of Iraq, the former venerable Naqib of Baghdad,[10] and pre-eminently the late King Faisal, such personalities evoked in those who met them the warmest feelings of personal friendship.

Anyone who had the privilege of meeting and talking to the late King Faisal must have come under the spell of his fascinating and magnetic personality.

That great lady, Gertrude Bell, was certainly not impervious to the charm of the Arab. In her conversation, in her private correspondence and official reports, her personal predilections took the form of an almost boundless exaggeration of Iraq's capacity for independence. Everything was couleur de rose to her at that time.

Not unnaturally, the Arabs – who are not only charming but also astute – gave these compliments a practical turn. From 1922 onwards, the British Government was confronted with an unceasing and increasing demand for cessation of tutelage and the abandonment of the mandate. The demand was logical; it was insistent; and it was successful. The initial steps had been too hasty, and the logical culmination could not be postponed. The political and administrative capacity of many individual Iraqis is very marked, but no one could feel at that time that Iraq as a country had the stability, the internal unity, the financial credit or the military strength to fulfil the rôle of an independent State in the only meaning of the term which the League of Nations or the civilized world could attach to it. The Mandates Commission of the League certainly did not accept that claim, and its weakness must have been apparent to those British authorities who at that time, in 1932, vouched for Iraq, and on whose sole responsibility and guarantee the League admitted her.

The hands of those authorities were tied at the time, tied by the exuberance with which the claims to independence had been originally fostered and canvassed in the early days. To have put the brake on in 1932 might have had a very disturbing effect.

The fruits of over-haste, over-confidence and incompatible aims were not long in appearing. The protection of minorities had been our especial care. The Assyrian massacre in 1933 was one of the earliest transactions of the new State, and it was then that the Iraq Army first felt its power. King Faisal, who had for ten years negotiated his country's independence with a remarkable sagacity and statesmanship seems somehow to have lost authority when formal independence had been attained. Perhaps it was the case that the dual task to which he was committed, of championing Iraq's independence and of keeping on good terms with his British patrons, was too much for him – (just as five years earlier, it had driven to suicide that very distinguished and honourable Prime Minister, Abdul Muhsin es Sa'dun) and Faisal died at Geneva in 1933, less than a year after the country had attained its formal independence, an irreparable loss and calamity to his country and to the policy of the British Government.

Deterioration set in after his death. His son and successor, the late King Ghazi, had no personal qualities for constitutional rule. The authority of Government had no stable foundation in the country. Tribal risings, which were always a possibility, but had hitherto been held in check by Faisal's personal ascendancy over the Sheikhs, broke out in 1934 and 1935, and the Iraqi Army again came into prominence. In 1936 occurred the first of those military coups d'état, which were to become chronic in succeeding years. Anti-British feeling grew and culminated in 1941, when, after prolonged indications of pro-Axis leanings the Government and Army of Rashid Ali declared openly for Germany and entered into hostilities with the British forces.

Such were the fruits of our policy. We found a country, recently liberated from its former masters, with a strong personality of its own, with a taste for material prosperity, and with a feeling of friendship for its British benefactors. We see it now – I refer, as I said, to the period up to 1941 – with minority problems more acute than under the tolerant Ottoman regime, with an elaborate, burdensome and expensive government, with no stable elements in the community to support it, and with the old rivalry between tribal and urban areas even stronger than in Turkish days, and, worst of all, with its former friendship for the British grievously impaired.

I call that a failure of policy, and that is why I say that the revision of policy is necessary.

Well, what can be done? I can only make a very brief suggestion, on very general lines. We cannot walk out, of course, even if there were any reason for that, we have incurred responsibilities, and we must discharge them. But there are two facts to be borne in mind, and one is that after the war the Allied Nations will be in a very strong position with regard to all small States. Neutrality has been of no use during the war; it has been a complete illusion. These small States have to come within the orbit of those powers which, after the war, must devise some system for the securing of the peace of the world. It follows then that military arrangements will have to fit into the international scheme.

The second fact is the existence of the Anglo-Iraq Treaty of 1930. I do not know how much of that treaty remains, or how far its provisions may have been infringed by recent happenings, but it does not seem to me to be of very much consequence to go into that. The main feature of that Treaty – which is a friendly alliance between Great Britain and Iraq – remains intact, though it may be necessary to make changes in detail in the relations between the two countries.

But the Iraq Army has proved a disturbing political fact and should go. There will be no scope for it in the new scheme. Any armed forces will have to form a part of the international system, and Iraq's share should be determined with reference to the need for developing her natural resources, that is, a sound financial and economic policy should be the principal aim.

We ought to take our relations with Iraq for a time and as far as possible out of the range of diplomacy. That Imperial policy to which I alluded a moment ago, viz full development of the resources of the Empire, should be applied to the case of Iraq also. Any country producing grain or other raw material will have to work overtime for many years after the war, and the development of irrigation, agriculture and communications, coupled with a genuine land settlement, should be the primary purpose of our policy.

That is, I think, the surest way of reviving something like the glories of past ages, and that is our only justification for our action in having separated Iraq from her historic connections and brought her into a false position of isolation. *(Applause.)*

Discussion

THE CHAIRMAN: I congratulate Mr. Slater on a masterly summary. He said a great deal one has waited to hear said, which has not been said.

There was one point which I have felt very much in the last two years, and that is that many of the points we have heard to-day are talked of in other countries. We sometimes tend to discuss our cases as if they were watertight; they are not. The political discussion going on now is very wide and very vital, and it should be borne in mind.

MR. CACCIA:[11] I should perhaps say, to start with, what I am not going to talk about, and what I am not even entitled to talk about, as being an official from the Foreign Office, and that is, either to attempt to defend the policy pursued in the past or to talk of anything that might suggest a line of policy in the future. Really not only would that be improper, but also it would be a waste of time, because an official should come here to hear what other people are thinking and not just to air his own ideas. So I am not going to talk about those things.

Secondly, it is against the general rule of my Office in any case to be allowed to address a meeting at all, and I have only obtained a somewhat reluctant approval of saying a few words to-day, so that I would beg that anything I may say should be regarded as strictly confidential and should not be quoted as the views of the Foreign Office, or quoted indeed at all.

There were three bases of Mr. Slater's most interesting and provocative talk which I should like to question; and in the subsequent discussion, I think that not only shall we hear ideas based on his assumptions but also on the opposite.

He said that our Imperial interests will no longer require that Great Britain should have a predominant position in the Middle East after the war. Frankly, I just do not agree. We have two interests in the Middle Eastern area: one is communications, and the other is oil.

To take the last alone, there are only three large oil producing areas in the world. One is in the possession of the Russians, and one in the possession of the Americans. That leaves a third, in which we shall have for a prolonged period the predominant interest of the really Great Powers.

What is more, if the war goes in the way in which at present the Prime Minister indicated it probably would with us, with the first collapse of Germany and Italy, followed by a period of war with Japan, our interests in the Middle East will be of a predominant character. Therefore that is the first assumption I should challenge. I should say we should have a predominant interest of the Great Powers in that area.

Secondly, Mr. Slater said in the course of his lecture that the defence of various areas would no doubt have to be guaranteed with some international system. That may be true, but I think it would be a very rash assumption to take for granted that the other Great Powers will be prepared to take a larger share than we in the defence of an area in which it is we rather than they that have the predominant interest on account of oil. That, of course, hangs with the previous assumption. If you assume that we have a predominant position in this area, then we shall have to pay for it in the matter of defence. You cannot have security guaranteed by other people; in fact, you have to work your way, if you intend to remain a Great Power.

Last of all as regards the financial position of these countries in the Middle East after the war. It will not be so much that they will be impoverished, but that they will hold large sterling and dollar balances and will want to spend them, and it may be in a period of the war – if it continues for Japan for a short time after the German war is finished – that it will be very difficult for them to find the actual materials to carry out the various development schemes which in their own interests will be desirable.

That brings us back again to the second point. Do you really think in this post-war system that national armies will be prepared to abolish themselves and act only in accordance with the dictates of some world Council? They may, but if present indications are anything to go on, I think that would be a very rash assumption to proceed upon, and therefore in any remarks made afterwards, I hope that some of them will be based on the opposite assumptions on all those three points: (1) that we have a predominant interest; (2) that therefore we shall have to bear the major burden of seeing that the area is protected; and (3) that on the whole those countries will have in the immediate post-war era money to spend rather than to have to look to their economy.

THE CHAIRMAN: I am very grateful for that touch of official realism. On the first point, I do think it is worth remembering that, even though Imperialism may be used in a gathering like this, it probably wants re-defining and explaining to the man in the street both here and in Baghdad.

COLONEL NEWCOME: Both speakers agreed that our communications in the Middle East are the main things that are concerned. Now in my view the things we really want are absolute security for the Suez Canal, absolute security Haifa to Basra, which means to say the Persian Gulf. Why? Because we have sea power, and have to have power to enforce law whether it is civil law or international law. You have to have sufficient power to control those communications. Outside that I do not see what on earth we have to do with whether Iraq has an army or not. Give those people the greatest independence you can, provided we coordinate with them in every other way. We have to have those communications secure. They know perfectly well that they cannot stand up for themselves, that they have to fall back on a Power for their own defence; as Ja'far often said: "For goodness' sake, move your army out of Iraq, but don't go too far, for Iran might come in to-morrow, or Turkey." You can tell them they should not have an army, if you tell them Iran and Turkey are not going to have armies. They must have something to withhold the shock until we can come behind them to support them. Let them have the greatest independence; they will grow up in ten or twenty years gradually.

Egypt has not suffered nearly as much as we used to think in 1922. Egypt has done much better than any of us said they would. I do not say it is perfect: but I do say, stick to these communications. Let them know what we want. That is the point. Let the Arabs know what we want. That is, we want those communications absolutely secured; and we want to coordinate with them, and they want our support. The more we let them have independence, cooperating with us, the better; and I should leave all other details alone.

THE CHAIRMAN: I do think that turns on the point I have in mind, and that is the difficulty in explaining.

A MEMBER: How can anybody maintain that Iraq or any other state could afford an army such as it had – simply a means of ambition for a small clique? That is what it came to.

MR. SLATER: May I say a word about that question Mr. Caccia raised, about Imperial interests. When I talked about Imperial interests, I deliberately said nothing about oil or air communications, because with regard to oil I knew somebody would mention it, and so I thought I would shorten my talk in that way.

But with regard to oil, the point I have in mind is this, that oil in Iraq is already an international interest. The concession for the working of the oil field in Iraq has been concluded between the Iraq Government and a very strong international group of oil interests on terms very favourable to the Iraq Government. There is no reason whatever to suppose that if we were to abandon our predominant position in the Middle East, the oil concession would collapse.

With regard to the air routes I do not know so much, but I believe it is very much to the interest of a State like Iraq to have air routes going through it. After all, they are concerned with tourist traffic, and money being brought into the country, so that there would be no difficulty whatever in maintaining those air routes, even if we were to drop any idea of military security. As regards military security, we established a strong military force or influence when there was a danger; when the danger receded, we withdrew it. For a long time we had no military predominance in that area.

Mr. Caccia said Iraq could afford an army. I think there are a lot of other things it could spend its money on better. One of them is communications on a very big scale, and irrigation on a really well thought out scale.

Two really well thought out irrigation schemes and communications are going to absorb all the money which the Iraq Government derives at present mainly from the oil companies.

I think that I have made some sort of very unsatisfactory answer to Col. Newcome about securing air communications. I believe they will secure themselves. It is to the interest of the people there. I am not sure also that these post-war arrangements will not include some provision for altering sovereignty in the air, and that, as far as transit over various territories is concerned, that is sure to be internationalized.

With regard to the right to interfere with the Iraq army, of course, the Iraq Government naturally would certainly say, "How dare you touch our army?" But the reason I recommended that was that it has been misused and abused. It is a disturbing and disintegrating factor. It would be in their own interest. How it would be done, I do not know, and I cannot undertake to say. That is a hard nut for somebody to crack, but not for me.

That, I say, is the line of policy that we should pursue, – to get them to give up the one factor in their constitution which has hitherto upset the internal prosperity and happiness of the country.

Col. Newcome showed a very forgiving spirit with regard to the Iraq army. There is no guarantee that it would always support the cause of the right, nor would it ever be of sufficient strength and size to meet any real external dangers.

MR. PETERS: I consider that the Iraq army has been the major cause of most of our troubles since 1933. First of all, it has absorbed at least 40 per cent of the revenue of the country, which, as Mr. Slater has intimated, might have been diverted into useful channels, irrigation and communications.

In these years from 1933 until date, we have had very few major irrigation projects. We had the Key Barrage, costing £2,000,000, and the Habbaniya Escape,[12] a portion of which has been completed and the rest is now under construction. These are the only major projects which have been completed since 1933. The one cry in the country has been for the glorification of the army.

As soon as they got into the League of Nations in 1932, conscription was soon introduced, and our hothouse bred nationalism was such that the country or townspeople as a whole in Baghdad and Basra paraded the streets like primitive savages with staves, swords and so on, to show their enthusiasm for the introduction of conscription. The conscript army started with a glorious start, and with this glorious start it never looked back. King Faisal himself was not far behind in promoting this conscript army to be a force of some considerable dimensions.

We have to admit that Abdul Muhsin, the Prime Minister who committed suicide in 1929, and King Faisal, who almost died of a broken heart in 1933, really died because they were disappointed with their own countrymen. I remember meeting Sheik _____ and he told me he had had a meeting with King Faisal on a certain island, and the king had given up almost the hope for any future for Iraq. The Iraq army had got out of hand with the Assyrians, and he found that, with the Iraq army getting loose, a number of other elements in the country had also got loose to shake his own existence.

From that time the Iraq army senior officers found their opportunity to mix in politics, and political leaders themselves also went into cooperation with these senior officers and the army time after time during the last few years since 1933 has upset all stable government.

I would remind you too of the incident from the disturbances which might have been of a very serious nature last year. The perpetrators behind the whole scheme were the four army leaders, and although Rashid Ali encouraged these people in their intrigues, in the end Rashid Ali was actually driven out by the army. The army had complete control of the place, and Rashid Ali was a tool in their hands.

Pasha _____ has been a tool. Even _____ himself has been in power at various times as the result of the army behind him. It has been openly admitted that, unless the Prime Minister at any time has the army behind him, he cannot proceed for very long. The result is that a Prime Minister comes along. Army officers are dismissed, others are promoted, others put on the shelf for the time being, and a system goes on which is a vicious one. It will be hopeless while this conscript army remains in Iraq. After the conclusion of the disturbance, the spirit of the country among the intelligentsia and others was that the army should be abandoned. The spirit was then existing, that the Iraq army had so miserably performed in that incident against a few thousand troops, that it was not worthy of maintenance and should be abolished.

Unfortunately we had an armistice. The country was not, as you know, brought to its knees. We had other commitments. We had Syria. We had a nasty position in Iran, and could not keep these hostilities proceeding longer than necessary, and therefore offered the Iraqi an armistice. The terms of the armistice were that the Iraqi army would be left, so it was left. In recent months new equipment has been given. Equipment has been diverted from the British army, and the Iraqi army has been resuscitated and re-equipped.

The spirit in the Iraq army is very little different. The general staff and the senior officers are those sympathetic to our cause, but down below among the regimental officers the spirit had not changed up to the time of the turn of events in North Africa.

The army have been a very disturbing influence in the country. They have removed some of the best administrators _____ Pasha was one of the finest administrators the country ever had. Faisal would have been living very probably to-day if the spirit of the Iraq army had not changed, and until that Iraq army ceases to exist, I maintain that we shall not have any political stability in Iraq.

They had a voluntary army previously, and I believe it was quite a fine institution. In order to appease their national aspirations, they might be permitted to have a small voluntary army, but preferably none at all. The purpose of the Iraq army is to deal with internal dissension. It is not concerned officially with an external aggressor, because the treaty with Britain is such that we offer for the period of thirty years to defend her against any external aggressor.

In any case, whatever army Iraq could get, would be no useful force to tackle Turkey. Turkey is her strongest neighbour. Ibn Saud was always a matter of great concern to them, but even the forces of Ibn Saud would not be a serious menace to them. Their main enemy would be Turkey, but I cannot consider in any case that Iraq should keep an army merely for the sake of attending to any aggression from Turkey.

The next point, which does not seem to have been referred to by Mr. Slater, is the question of Palestine. A disturbing influence which has assisted the Axis throughout these years in Iraq is this Palestine question. Some people may argue that Iraq is not sufficiently interested in Palestine. All I can say to that is that Britain's enemies will always use the Palestine problem as a means of undermining Iraq, and it has been done very successfully so far.

In 1938 _____ made his position very clear. He told the German Legation that they would be expected to get out within twenty-four hours after the declaration of war. Later the position deteriorated very seriously. The Mufti who came over played a great part in the positioning[?] of Rashid Ali and the others. We must realize that the Palestine question cannot be treated aside from Iraq. It must be settled before we can expect any political stability in Iraq.

Mr. C[hairman] I have not much to add to what has been said, speaking as a private individual, but I do sympathise very much with everything that has been said against the rôle of the Iraq army in the past. I should have doubted whether it was worth making any first-class political issue out of the question. If it is true that a small army is no longer of any use at all in the present state of mechanized warfare, the Iraqis may come themselves to see that it is really not worth their while spending so large a proportion of their income on it.

Why is the Iraq army a menace? Surely because of the strong nationalist feeling in Iraq. Unless some way is found of mitigating the anti-British feeling in Iraq, merely to impose by force or diplomacy the diminution of the army would increase the feeling of frustration.

THE CHAIRMAN: You admit anti-British feeling. Cannot we possibly have an account as to the origins of that, and why? This discussion is about post-war Britain.

MR. CROSSWAYS: I should like to hear Col. Newcombe on that.[13] I do not think one can put it all down to Palestine.

Undoubtedly it is partly a survival of feeling; first of all, of strong objection to the Imperialist policy pursued in the immediate war and post-war period; and partly to the feeling that we did not go fast enough. They did not want British people about at all and thought we were not going fast enough, and that the Treaty policy was a fraud and would leave us just as powerful as we were before.

COLONEL NEWCOME: In 1938 I was travelling down to Baghdad in a car with an ordinary Iraq railway engineer. He said, "We are awfully happy with you. Everything is going well. We are developing our army and doing well with our railway. But why on earth are you going on with this Palestine policy? You are breaking up all our arrangements on account of Palestine."

In 1940 I went out again [. . . .] ——— wrote me a letter which he handed to me personally, saying, "We have four Committees in Baghdad, four in Damascus, Committees in Afghanistan, Persia, all over Egypt. All these people are contributing funds to us. The German propaganda is about ten per cent of the trouble. The real trouble is ourselves; we are prejudiced through the mistakes made on the Palestine question. If you will remove the fear of Zionist domination, we will stop our anti-British propaganda and cooperate with you." I may over-estimate the Palestine case, but the feeling was very strong, and they were using that tremendously as a lever.

THE CHAIRMAN: That is the version I have heard elsewhere.

Mr. CROSSWAYS: I think that, quite apart from the Palestine question, we would have very much the same trouble. The fact is that we want to have certain interests protected, and to take a certain fatherly control, not always disinterested, in what goes on there. That must lead to political difficulties, and how they can be mitigated, I do not know. To say that it is all due to Palestine, or even fifty per cent of it, I think is wrong.

THE CHAIRMAN: There is one point that has come out between our two official speakers to-day. On the one hand we were assured that Imperialism in its very best sense is to continue after this war, as against Mr. Salter's more mitigated statement.

MR. CROSSWAYS: It might be United Nations Imperialism.

THE CHAIRMAN: That does not matter from the point of view of these wretched people living in these countries.

It seems to me it has now come to the point as to whether we can assure them of our intentions, or whether we are going to go through the process that happened after the last war. It is true that we have come out of it fairly well. Most of what we said we would do, we have done, but there is still distrust.

MR. PRICE: With regard to Palestine, I understand that most of the retail trading is in the hands of Jews for the whole of the Arab world. Is that incorrect? The point I was going to raise is that, if you take up an anti-Jewish policy, would you not have rather bad economic effects on some of the areas under control. If you admitted an anti-Jewish policy, you might upset the economic conditions.

THE CHAIRMAN: I do not think so.

MR. PRICE: The second point was about the grain production in Iraq. We have to bear in mind the probable overproduction of grain in the world.

MR. SLATER: Iraq is not, of course, an important source of grain production at all relatively with other parts of the world. But I am astonished that it should be suggested that any country could afford to do less than its utmost in grain production for some years after this war. The quality of the grain is not particularly good, but a certain amount of time and money might very well be spent on improving the quality.

A MEMBER: Surely there would be a great risk if we had an over-production, and then found it was no longer required?

THE CHAIRMAN: That is academic, considering there is an over-shortage now.

MR. SLATER: I gathered that the speaker thought the Iraqis had some grievance at not having sufficient independence. I must say, I think, if that is so, they are extraordinarily greedy.

MR. CROSSWAYS: But why should they not be? Everybody is.

MR. SLATER: I did not suggest, I hope, any diminution or derogation of Imperialism, but a different kind of imperial interest.

MR. BOWMAN: I should like to say one thing on Col. Slater's extraordinarily interesting address, and that is that three-fourths of it was hastily leading up to the fact that our policy was fundamentally wrong in giving Iraq its independence in 1931 or 1932. It was actually given in 1930, and the League of Nations in 1932. He explained very clearly and lucidly, and I am sure perfectly correctly, the reason which led up to that, and then said that our policy was wrong.

Personally I have been in the fortunate position of being able to watch Iraq at fairly close quarters for a great many years. Col. Slater and I chanced to go there a good many years ago, and afterwards I was not so far away. Gertrude Bell was a great friend of mine and wrote me many letters, and we met from time to time up to the day of her death. Sir Percy Cox and Wilson were also very close personal friends.

I believe now, looking back on all those years, that our policy was right. If we had not done as we did, there were only two alternatives: one was to clear out bag and baggage, and the other was to remain in force. We know what the result of remaining in force is from our experience elsewhere. I need not mention Palestine. I do not want to drag in Palestine, but we know what the trouble has been there, and the trouble has only been suppressed by force, leaving bitterness behind.

The same in Egypt on a good many occasions, notably in 1919.

In Iraq on the whole it has not worked out so badly. There has been trouble with Rashid Ali, and lots of people do not like us; but I do not think that that need deter us from future experiments of the same kind. I am very much of a Liberal in these matters, and I should like to think that the Royal Central Asian Society was also Liberal in these matters.

I do not in the least wish to detract from the enormous importance of our Imperial communications.

Sir K[inahan] Cornwallis has done wonders in the last few years. He knows the people; he knows them all, and he knows how to deal with them. If we send our proper envoys, and a few and very carefully selected British officials, who are the right type, I do not believe we shall have any trouble at all. I believe very largely that the trouble not only in Iraq but elsewhere as been partly because we have sent out the wrong kind of man, and partly because we have not always treated the people, whom we are helping to govern, absolutely in the right way.

I would like to repeat that the policy, I believe, was right, and I believe that the future of Iraq is not nearly so black as it has been painted this afternoon.

SIR PERCY SYKES: I have listened to all the lectures on all these subjects, and I agree with the last speaker that our policy was right. I consider Sir Percy Cox a very great man, who carried it through with his personality.

About the army, surely when things have settled down, they can make it into a smaller force. Because you have always to remember that the Kurds are a troublesome people.

I think to-day's discussion is the best I have ever listened to.

MR. SLATER: I have not got very much to say. The last sentence of Sir Percy Sykes disarmed any observations that anybody could make. I tried to give a clear, and I hope a fairly correct and well-balanced picture of what had been the result of the policy. I did not try to be too a priori in dealing with it.

When you are talking about independent States, I think you have to try and draw a distinction between those States that have had an historical independence and which for some reason or other have come under different conditions, and the case of starting an entirely new State.

In Iraq we are making a gratuitous experiment. It never has been a State, and never can become a real self-contained State.

As regards its defence, the police should be sufficient. Sir Percy Sykes suggested that the troubles it might have from Kurds could be adequately dealt with by the police, and that was the intention from the beginning. The army has proved a danger.

We have such influence there; we have such power; we have an Ambassador and a large number of people out there in an advisory capacity. They should exercise their responsibilities and not merely sit there; they should influence, direct and guide the policy. That is why I think it would be possible, without doing any violence to the Iraq sense of prestige and amour propre to modify the policy which has been dominant, which was a daring and on the whole an unsuccessful experiment.

I hope that it is not thought that I did not attach sufficient value to the work done by those who were responsible for the setting up of this wonderful experiment – Sir Percy Cox particularly. I did not wish to dwell on those things because I had to make my remarks as brief as possible. But nobody could have a greater admiration for the knowledge, skill and sagacity with which he carried out that task.

THE CHAIRMAN: I have learned a lot of history, but I have not been reassured with regard to the barrage of questions with which I shall be faced when I return shortly.

They are disturbed. Our policy is not clear to them.

When Mr. Bowman says that we hope our diplomatic representation will be better, I, being concerned with Universities for twenty years and at the present time, do not see the slightest sign of the training other countries have given, being set on foot in this country.

If it is felt that we want better representation, we shall have to do something about it. For instance, the removal of the School of Oriental Studies and its Library might be considered in this association.

Notes

1 Colonel Slater C.M.G.,C.I.E was one of the men who produced '*Iraq – Report on Iraq Administration. October 1920–March 1922* a highly detailed report looking at every aspect of British administration in the country. He was the British Advisor to the Finance and Commerce ministries of the government of Iraq. He was dismissed in 1924 supposedly for being too pro-Iraqi. See *Inventing Iraq,* by Toby Dodge (2003).

2 General Francis Rawdon Chesney (1789–1872), soldier and explorer, investigated the feasibility of a canal from Port Said to Suez, which was subsequently realised by Ferdinand de Lesseps in 1869 as the Suez Canal.

Chesney also explored an overland route to India, firstly by steamer along the river Euphrates and later through the Euphrates valley railway scheme, which although approved by the House of Commons, was not taken up.

3 With the granting of independence to the Indian sub-continent in 1947, the whole raison d'etre of Britain's Middle East policy, to defend India, was negated. Oil supplies now became the primary focus.

4 Gertrude Bell (1868–1926), British traveller, archaeologist, and political officer in the Middle East.

5 King Faisal I was a son of the Grand Sherif of Mecca, hence the term 'shereefian'.

6 Sir Percy Cox, a colonial administrator and first High Commissioner at Baghdad in the 1920s.

7 Sir Arnold Wilson, predecessor to Sir Percy Cox and civil commissioner in Baghdad 1918–1920.

8 Hedjaz, or Hejaz, along Saudi Arabia's western coast, was ruled by the Hashemite Sherif of Mecca from 1916 to 1925.

9 Jafar al-Askari, twice prime minister of Iraq in the 1920s.

10 The first prime minister of Iraq.

11 Sir Harold Caccia (1905–1990), diplomat, ambassador, chair of Joint Intelligence Committee

12 The Habbaniya Escape, a flood prevention measure, an artificial weir.

13 Colonel S.F. Newcombe gave the last lecture in this series 'A Forecast of Arab Unity' in late 1943, early 1944. See page 000.

LECTURE FOUR

Persia

By Christopher Sykes
Lecture on 10 November 1943

Introduction

In 1907 Britain and Russia signed the Anglo-Russian Convention in an attempt to end the 'Great Game' that had been played out for nearly a century between the two major powers. Russia was pushing southwards, overcoming independent khanates like Khiva, while Britain anxiously guarded India and had suffered two major defeats in Afghanistan. The Convention, among other things, divided Persia into three parts, the northernmost section under Russian control, the southeast under Britain and a neutral zone across the middle of the country. Persia was at that time ruled by the Qajar dynasty and it was their inability to prevent Russian and British control that led to a coup by an army officer, Reza Khan. Khan was nominated by the Persian National Assembly as monarch, and became Reza Shah Pahlevi, ruling from 1925 to 1941.

The Shah carried out radical reforms to modernise Persia through a strong, centralised government. He constructed the Trans-Iranian railway, linking Teheran with the Persian Gulf. He did not employ Russian or British aid, although Britain owned the oil rights, through its Anglo-Persian Oil Company, started in 1913. At the outbreak of World War Two, Iran, as the country was now called, tried to remain neutral. However, the Shah refused to expel his German technicians and this led to an Anglo-Russian invasion in September 1941, which saw the Shah forced to abdicate in favour of his son and go into exile. Sykes describes Persia under Reza Shah as a 'fascist regime,' an exaggerated response to a country which had been under Anglo-Russian influence for years. Early in 1942 America offered to send in advisors to administer Persia and to support Russia and Britain, thus adding a third foreign element.

Sykes' lecture is a justification for British action in Persia, which was not surprisingly resented by the Persians, although he tries to put a gloss on it. Britain's prestige fell even further with the offer of American aid. The lecturer, who subsequently had a successful career as an author and broadcaster thought the BBC and the British Council could do more to win over Persian opinion, particularly by making English literature available and British histories of Persia by Sir Percy Sykes, who was chairing the lecture, and Lord Curzon.

PRIVATE AND CONFIDENTIAL
ROYAL CENTRAL ASIAN SOCIETY
Report of a Meeting
held at 8 Clarges Street, London W1
on Wednesday, November 10th, 1943
Chairman: Brig.-General Sir Percy Sykes, KCIE, CB, CMG
Christopher Sykes lecturing[1]

THE CHAIRMAN: Ladies and Gentlemen, When I first visited Constantinople, some fifty odd years ago, the Englishman who was well-known there as a traveller was the grandfather of our lecturer, Sir Christopher Sykes. All the guides and people said, "Of course, you are a relation of his." I replied, "Oh no, I am a very poor individual, no relation whatever," otherwise I should have been ruined with baksheesh and gifts.

Then his father, Sir Mark Sykes, was better known for his work in Turkey, about which he wrote books, and he did political work too. But he also visited Persia. Now we come to the grandson, Christopher Sykes. Christopher Sykes, after the last war, visited Persia, studied it very earnestly, and came to the conclusion that one of the most interesting figures there was Wassmuss,[2] the man who helped to arrange for my being [held hostage] for about six weeks. So he went and stayed with the robber barons, and collected all their horrible tales of what they were going to do with me when they caught me.

He then with Robert Byron, a most brilliant young man whose death we all deplore – I deplore it enormously because I admired him so much – did the road to Oxiana, which was more than it appears because they travelled all over Northern and Eastern Persia, Robert Byron being an AI archaeologist. They even visited all the important sites in Afghanistan, so that was an extraordinary piece of work. Together – it is supposed to be a great secret – they wrote a book called "Innocence and Design." It was a dead secret, of course, but I looked at the illustrations, and I remembered that Sir Mark was a very skilful caricaturist, so I said, "This must be his work," and so it was.

Mr. Christopher Sykes has now been some time at Teheran, doing valuable work and getting to know a good deal about the country, and I will now call on him to address us. *(Applause.)*

MR. CHRISTOPHER SYKES: I must thank you very much, Mr. Chairman, for your kind remarks, but I must admit that, in spite of what you have been good enough to say about me, in speaking under this title I feel somewhat like a man who, having heard of electrons that morning, is billed to give a lecture on atomic structure that afternoon. I recognize that the subject is an immense one, and in order to impose decent limits on myself, I wish to confine my remarks to the political situation of Great Britain in Persia at the present time. I must admit my limitations. Apart from the fact, of which I would not be so impertinent as to remind this Society, that Persia is a vast and complex subject, my views have been latterly influenced by a fairly long residence in Teheran, but a short residence, in comparison, in the Persian provinces.

It is true that Persia is now a highly centralized state; but no matter how unassailably that proposition may apply to matters of administration, the opinion, and thus the political bases of Persia, remain as wildly local and restricted as they did a hundred years ego. A friend of mine in Persia summed this matter up neatly once by saying that Teheran was universally acknowledged throughout Persia as the administrative and spiritual centre of the country, but that he had never once known Teheran influence the provinces, in opinion, nor the provinces influence Teheran. To be estimated as a whole, Persia must be known as a whole. Having depressed you with a recital of my limitations, permit me now, before we go farther, to excite your confidence with a list of my advantages. It is a short list. I speak the language fluently but ungrammatically. My greatest linguistic boast is that I was once mistaken for a Persian in the heart of Kurdistan. I know many Persians, and I think I may assert that in my Persian acquaintance I have some intimate friends who tell me without any reserve what they feel about their own country, and how Great Britain appears to a Persian scrutiny. I would only add in this rather vulgar recital of my qualifications, that I knew Persia with some intimacy during the tyranny of Reza Shah and again after his fall.

Apart from the unique situation of Great Britain in Persian affairs, the Persian subject has a compelling interest. It is often overlooked that Persia provided the first example in this war of the fall of a fascist regime. Two years before we were confronted with the present events in Italy, we were dealing with parallel problems in mid-Asia. It may be objected that Oriental despotism and European fascism are very different things. I believe that this view pays too much respect to local peculiarities and too little to the uniformity of human nature. When I consider the adoption of parliamentary practice by Persia, with what devotion and enthusiasm this was accomplished, the passion for advancement in modern progress which shook the country from the late nineteenth century to the post-war years, how disillusion and inexperience were used as the pretext for the revival of older, more familiar and more barbaric systems, the parallel between fascism and the Pahlevi autocracy seems to me almost exact. The difficulties of the British position in Persia are prophetic of the difficulties awaiting us in expectant Europe. We should recognize that in Persia we have been provided with a hard and realistic school in which to learn. That, I think, is the first interest of Persia to us to-day.

The second which I propose to discuss is less general – more intimate. Persia has always been regarded as the key stone in the design of buffer-States. Whether we like it or not, the fact remains that on the day that Russian and British troops entered Persia, the whole fabric of that great political vision passed away, leaving not a wrack behind. Well, no. Perhaps a wrack or two did remain as an afterthought, and we will consider them later.

What position does Great Britain hold in Persia? An awkward one. We are the focal point of Persian hopes. We are the symbol of frustration, even of despair. Most concisely in the Persian imagination we are still summed up in the dread figure – 1907.[3] (By the bye, I met recently a British official in Persia who informed me he had never heard about what happened in 1907 and did not want to know, as he was anxious to get on with the war. You can imagine how successful his efforts were – in Persia at any rate – but let that pass.) The paradox of 1907 explains to Persians to-day the oddity of the English character. We tend, I think, to be complacent about our oddities. We think of them as amiable. To alien eyes they sometimes appear as diabolical. We should realize that.

England as the guardian of freedom, as the eternal foe of oppression, the organizer of liberty in the very camp and fortress of tyranny: this is a description of England's function in the world to which most Persians who are well disposed towards us, and many who are not, would willingly subscribe. Our fearless action in 1907, which obtained for Persia the machinery of representational Government, is by no means forgotten. But a less agreeable picture is also present to Persian eyes, both friendly and otherwise. We are equally imagined as subtle and cruelly selfish. As the people who did not scruple in that same year, 1907, to drive a bargain with Imperial Russia at Persia's expense, a people who were and still are prepared to trade noble principles in the

coarsest way of business. It says much for our reputation that the propaganda of Reza Shah, which was strangely supported by German
propaganda never succeeded in wholly obliterating the more pleasing
picture. And those two propagandas were main formative influences.
Reza Shah's propaganda was simple in method and intention.
England, so Persians were told, belonged to the past, to the vanished
house of the Kajars [Qajars],[4] to the strifes and excitements of a
vanished age. The aim of this hateful power was to reproduce the
miserable weakness of the old Persia, once more to enjoy her
unbounded influence among the poverty-stricken. German propaganda followed a line dissimilar only in one notable detail. England,
according to Dr. Goebbels's[5] theory, was the core and centre of an
expiring order of things. Her aim was to perpetuate reaction and
oppose progress. To serve her purpose she would go to astonishing
lengths to organize tyranny. England was not only the support but the
instigator, in detail, of the oppression of Reza Shah. Englishmen to-
day who, under the stress of the present turmoil, loudly regret the
"good old days" of Reza Shah's "firm hand" have as a rule little notion
how exactly they rise to Dr. Goebbels's fairest hopes. What was most
strange about this widely disseminated propaganda was that Reza
Shah never seems to have taken any action to suppress or to contra-
dict stories so damaging to his prestige. It is easy to see how his own
and German propaganda, though partly contradictory, were not
mutually effacing. The evoked image of Great Britain was consistent.

The conditioning factor in Persia to-day, from whatever angle she is
considered, is the fall of Reza Shah. Let us very briefly recollect what
that implied.

No one should deny that Reza Shah was a great man. No more
vigorous personality had occupied the Peacock throne since Nadir
Shah, nor one who left such enduring memorials of himself in Persia
since Abbas the Great. All the more tragic is it therefore, that this
remarkable sovereign should not have escaped from the limits of the
antique mould of tyranny and oppressive autocracy. He opened his
career as a reformer, but, lacking all superior moral qualities, he ended
as a reactionary who has done more than any other man to perpetuate
or at least prolong the days of Persian ignorance.

The key flaw in the mind and character of Reza Shah was that he
shared with so many of his subjects the abiding fault of the Persian
genius: superficiality. The closest friend of Iran[6] is unable to deny the
persistent tendency of superficiality in the art, the studies, and the
administration of the country, and from this fault the Shah was not
only unfree: he took it to unprecedented lengths. Hardly one of his
numerous reforms was not hasty and ill-considered. His reign must be

remembered for the building of many hospitals – without any advance in sanitation. Open drains still flank the new asphalted streets of Teheran. Remembered, too, for the adoption of European clothes and the limitation of all that was best in European influence, the closing of Persia's best foreign schools. New buildings built with the old unstable materials. Teheran to-day is one, perhaps the best planned and most artistic, of the new capitals of the East. Already the older of the recent buildings show signs of imminent collapse. His reign must be remembered as that of Persian independence and the degradation of the Persians by a renewed autocracy, of the patriot king who did not shrink from escaping blame by posing as a creature of the British Government.

The most calamitous of all Reza Shah's reforms was his attempt to ensure cheap bread for the population – an admirable intention but organized without the slightest reference to the local background of production. The result was that Persia lost an eighth, or as some people think, even a fifth of her cultivatable land. There may be a connection between this and the disastrous decline in the Persian population. The noise and the vigour with which this evil administration was proclaimed to be the expression and embodiment of all that was best in the Persian genius and the modern world, deceived a regrettably large number of foreign observers and Governments. They are not entirely without excuse. Reza Shah may yet receive the forgiveness and gratitude of posterity for two blessings. He was, I believe, the first Persian sovereign to preserve and restore the ancient artistic treasures of his country. He gave to Persia the inestimable boon of complete religious toleration. It is true that in his degeneracy he forsook this noble principle, but in the days of his vigour he has given an example which endured.

When the Shah abdicated, his most noticeable legacy to the country was an extreme shortage of basic supplies – and of men. It is difficult to say which was the more serious of these deficiencies. Perhaps that of men. To solve the supply problem the formation of a vigorous and courageous Government was the first essential, and this had to be found in a country in which those who had not grown up in fear, and particularly in fear of taking any responsibility, were now elderly men.

(A) How did Great Britain appear at this moment in Persian eyes? It is a sober statement of fact to say that in September and October of 1941 the hopes of all Persia were centred on Great Britain. The reasons may, I think, be classified as follows:

1. The Germans might never arrive.
2. Britain would protect the Persians from the Russians.

3. It was generally believed that British initiative had removed Reza Shah, and that as a logical consequence Great Britain would take over the Government.
4. There was a sudden impulse for freedom. 1907 was remembered again.

For reasons very difficult to determine, the Persians tend to under-estimate, or even to ignore, the political influence of Russia. Russia has not, it is true, exerted a great proportion of influence, compared to what she might do, but the fact that the presence of Russia is the grand conditioning factor in much of our Eastern policy, is rarely real-ized by Persians. I realize it is difficult to give an account of opinion such as the foregoing, which is not based on inadequate personal observation.

(B) Now how did Great Britain react to the difficult problem of boundless hopes centred on her and which, in the middle of a war, she was in no position to realize except in the meagrest, in the most disap-pointing manner? We can best describe the next episode in our policy as a revival of the anomaly of the last war: namely, that although Allied troops had taken up stations in North and South Persia, every effort was concentrated on maintaining the political integrity of Iran. The culmination of these first attempts to mitigate the shock of the inva-sion to Persian independence was the Anglo-Russian-Persian treaty of 1942.[7] Cynics described this policy as a burying of British heads in the sand; apologists pointed out that only by giving maximum support to the notion of Persian independence when it was weakest could we give undeniable proof of the sincerity of our often declared regard for the rights of nations.

At the time of which I am speaking, the early months of 1942, the Persians with few if any exceptions found themselves among the cynics. The argument ran somewhat as follows: "The problems of to-day are overwhelming. The Administration lacks prestige, experience and a popular vote, and it is called upon to organize food production, price control, internal order, and the conciliation of a liberated but needy population. Desirable as the removal of the tyranny undoubt-edly was, this action, which no amount of argument will persuade us was anything but a British action, has precipitated our crisis in the acutest form. We stand in need of something more tonic and dynamic than smiles of encouragement from the power which has landed us in this predicament, but smiles are all that England advances us in the hour of an extreme peril for which she is ultimately responsible."

Imagine variations, friendly, hostile, absurd and reasonable, of this theme, and you will have some idea of how Great Britain appeared to most Persians at this time. It was often pointed out that the abdication of Reza Shah was in no way accomplished by foreign powers, but was done on the personal decision of the monarch alone. I think, myself, that when we consider the effect on his subjects of the published protest to him by the British and Russian representatives, and of the famous denunciation of Reza Shah by the Persian Service of the B.B.C.[8] which preceded the abdication by a few days, we cannot refuse all share in the event.

Another oddity which may strike us is the fact that the appeal for administrative assistance should be addressed to us, so exclusively, and not first to Russia. Terror, panic terror of Russia was still common in Persia at that time. To this it must be added that the familiar misinterpretation of Russia by Persians was very evident too in this year. Exaggerations of the importance of our rôle carry with them a curious under-estimate of the Russian rôle in Persia. I have already mentioned this. Perhaps I may illustrate it by a curious example from my experience. I was in Khorassan in the first winter after the entrance of the troops. I asked a well-informed friend of mine whether the impeccable discipline of the Russian troops there had not greatly diminished the current terror and hatred of Russia in those provinces. He said that this effect had been much less than might have been supposed owing to a very general belief that the restraint of the Russians was due exclusively to the influence of the British Legation. I can only offer a lame explanation of the frequent Persian misrepresentation of Russia: that Russia is so vast and close a subject that the Persian imagination boggles before it. I have sometimes wondered what the verb "to boggle" means exactly, and perhaps in this context Persia supplies the answer.

I do not wish to imply that there was at any time a conflict or indeed any clear cut issue between Persia and Britain on this question. The truth was very different: it gradually became evident that Great Britain was not prepared to accept any deep political undertakings in this part of the world, and from having been the centre of extravagant and undefined hopes, Great Britain became the object of bitter and irrational disillusion. The dream of Great Britain as the power who could and wished to direct Persian destinies into new, healthy and free paths gave way, largely under the influence of the Berlin Radio, to a belief that Britain was to be identified with the ills and disorders of the new time, and the failures of the Foroughi[9] and the first Soheili administrations were generally ascribed to our inexplicable preference for reaction and incompetence. I would not be surprised to learn that we still appear in those ugly colours when we are viewed through Persian spectacles.

It was realized by us soon after the abdication that total non-interference in Persian affairs could in fact only serve selfish ends. The demand which accounted for extravagant misinterpretations, namely that Persia should receive a strong measure of Western assistance, was a just and proper one. The light measure of interference which Great Britain allowed herself in the appointment of additional consular officers to assist Governors in the inspection of wheat reserves and production, and in the Anglo-Persian Wheat scheme in the South of Persia, were recognized as wholly inadequate.

Then the best imaginable solution unexpectedly offered itself in the early spring of 1942. An intimation came from Washington to the effect that the Government of the United States was prepared to consider with favour any request from the Persian Government for the appointment of American advisors. Hope at last dawned that the mutual embarrassments of Russia and Great Britain were to be closed by a radical and effective innovation. Great Britain did all in her power to encourage the American scheme, and in the summer and autumn of the same year, American advisors were appointed to the main departments of the Persian administration. The situation of the country had grown desperate. The burning resentments of many years had exploded in revolts in the North, South and West, and were not made less difficult by the decline in authority and prestige of the Persian Government and by the over-sensitive aloofness to the inner affairs of the country shown throughout this period by Russia and Great Britain. In moments of acute distress the minds of men, particularly the minds of imaginative men such as the Persians, tend to fantasy and dreams. As soon as the American appointments were announced, miracles, immediate and all-redeeming miracles were expected. That the miracles did not materialize was quickly and instinctively attributed to obstacles set in the path of the advisors by Great Britain. This incident, which I am careful not to exaggerate, may give some idea of the depths to which our reputation has sunk in Persia. We are right back where we started.

There seems no doubt that, given time, a continuity of policy in the United States, and the acquirement of experience, the American experiment in Persia will succeed. When it is considered how vitally important to us is the stability of Persia, every Englishman should feel gratitude to America for having undertaken this difficult and selfless task and for providing the only solution to an extremely obstinate political problem. In the light of the new prospects which this turn of events offers, how can we best solve our personal problem? How can we conjure away the hideous caricature of ourselves which has so persistently taken shape in the imagination of Persians, and retrieve our old position as the sure support of progress and reform? If I offer some suggestions now, I do not do so in a spirit of omniscience but impressed by what has been forced on my observation while living in Persia and by exchanges of ideas with Persians.

In two respects the theory of buffer states should not be allowed to become a sacred axiom of our policy. In two respects it is out of date. A typical invention of the nineteenth century conception of nationality, it ignores the interdependence of different groups and interests which appears so much more vividly as a result of painful experience to a modern political philosophy. That is the general and deeper objection. We English have also a private one. The theory was first conceived before the Anglo-Persian Oil Company[10] had become as great a factor in affairs as it now is. The Company is now so large an item in the national economy and must maintain Great Britain in so prominent a posture before the eyes of Persia that a total withdrawal of British political influence would hardly be possible, no matter how desirable such a withdrawal might be. That being so, and I cannot believe that such a proposition is open to serious dispute, let us not refuse our fences. Let our influence be definite and inspired. We believe that we are on the verge of an era of intimate Anglo-American collaboration. Let us determine to make Persia the scene of model collaboration.

We had no slight share in the establishment of civil liberties in Persia. The Madjliss[11] is the direct offspring of the British Houses of Parliament. Now I think that no Persian and no Englishman would contest the statement that Parliamentary Government in Persia has proved a failure up to date – a complete and disastrous failure. Surely we have some obligation, as the founders of liberty in Persia, to assist in a regeneration of democracy in that country. We share in the errors of that frustrated parliamentary rule. We were guided by our own history and the history of England, to the confusion of its admirers, has the singular disadvantage of standing on its head. The speculation may be overbold, but I think it possible that modern social history in Britain may appear to future generations as the discovery of the importance of local authorities. Can we seriously blame a country of autocratic traditions because it failed with Parliamentarism when it was in no position to find out what were the true bases of representational Government: bases then but dimly suspected by the Mother of Parliaments and the Mentor of Persia. I think not. And I think further that to refuse now to take any part in the regeneration of freedom in Persia must mean that we deny the single character of freedom, and that we do not wholly or unreservedly believe in the things for which we are fighting. I sometimes wish that the British Council abroad would spend less time in explaining the beauties of Geoffrey Chaucer, and more time in urging the best way to preserve the freedom of the Parish Pump.

This brings me to another point. The tradition of British policy towards Persia is essentially a simple one. It is very easy to understand. And yet Britain has for a long time, and never more than now, appeared to Persians as a mysterious, a horribly and tortuously mysterious power. I cannot feel that this does anything but harm to us. It is quite unnecessary. The whole theory is all there and plain in our actions, for all to learn who wish to do so. Can we honestly say that we have put every facility in the way of the Persian reader? Apart from scholars of English, Persians know nothing of that large mass of English literature which deals with their country, and the familiar foreign idiom of Persia is predominantly French. It is safe to say that in consequence they know nothing of our policy in their country; they have to piece it together as best they may, and Berlin is always ready to lend a hand, a large powerful hand, for Berlin has, even now, an extremely persuasive radio. It is a pity that we do not help ourselves a little more plentifully with the B.B.C., that we do [not] use it to extol the roses of Shiraz (which the Persians regard as their own business anyway) or to indulge in flatteries which the shrewd Frenchmen of the East do not easily fall for, and not to explain confidently and in detail our intentions and our ideals, what we most strongly wish for and what we advise.

I understand that Sir Percy Sykes's *History*[12] is now in process of translation into Persian. Thus is welcome and most important news. It is to be hoped that it is a portent of a new trend, and perhaps I may be allowed to make a suggestion to this Society.

There is now a British Council in Persia.[13] Here surely, in spite of objections which I intend to mention, an opportunity offers of a cultural undertaking most necessary to our position: namely, the organized translation and publication in Persian of the most illuminating statements, official and un-official, of British political theory affecting the Middle East. I am thinking, for example, of the historic correspondence which took place between the British Government, Sir Percy Cox, and the Government of India in the year 1919; a correspondence, included in the Official History of the War in Persia, which more effectively than any other series of documents disposes of suspicions, which may remain, that our designs regarding Persia have an imperialistic flavour. Let me also urge that the Official History is translated. I will have your approbation, I hope, for thinking, most strongly of all, of Lord Curzon's great work. I do not suggest, indeed it would be most ill-advised, that Lord Curzon's "Persia"[14] should be translated verbatim, without any editing, and published at the most accessible price. I know that many of Lord Curzon's remarks on the Persian character are harsh, ungenerous, and deformed by a passion for generalization. But I do suggest that the whole theory of the "buffer state" is more clearly enunciated in this great work than in any other attempt which may be elsewhere found.

I propose that the British Council should make itself responsible for a twofold task: first, the compilation of a new up-to-date edition of "Persia and the Persian Question"; and, secondly, the publication of a commentary, an essay on Lord Curzon's connection with Persia, and on his still so vitally important book, written not for scholars but for the common reader, which, translated into Persian, may make those most nearly concerned familiar with a trend of policy, and with deviations from that trend, still so closely associated with Lord Curzon's name.

There are, I believe, technical objections to a republication of Lord Curzon's book on Persia. The task of bringing it up to date would in any case occupy some years. But I can see no objection why, in the meantime, the commentary should not be immediately undertaken.

It may be urged in objection that the British Council has a commitment to further our cause by cultural means, and that such a work as I have suggested has a political complexion. But surely there are certain high political concerns which are so intimately associated with the history of peoples that the only way in which they can be authentically expressed is through the culture of those people. I think that no one would deny that books such as Sir Percy Sykes's history and Lord Curzon's compilation belong to English literature, not only because they illustrate British literary ability, but also because they illustrate British ideas. 1 can conceive no more apt function for this Society than that it should furnish the British Council with the learning and the means to popularize such works as I have mentioned. I implied earlier that a vulgarization, in the French sense, of Lord Curzon's book in Persian might needlessly distress Persian readers. The commentary I have suggested might protect the English reader from following his prejudices. In any case, I suggest that a briefer version of the original work, such as the excellent abbreviation of "Arabia Deserta",[15] is necessary for Englishmen who are appointed to Persia, together with a vulgarization (again I use the word in its French sense), of such notable essays on our theme as Professor E. G. Browne's Reflections on the Persian Revolution of 1907, and a recasting of Sir Arnold Wilson's book on Persia, in the Modern World Series; a book of wonderful accuracy but requiring drastic revision.

We undergo a grave danger by neglecting to educate ourselves. I mentioned earlier a rather startling example of what I have in mind –

the British official who had not heard about 1907. Let us be clear what we are about. Let us see that every Englishman who goes to do service in Persia has some notion of our history and position there. Our worst disservice to ourselves is to render the perplexities which unhappily surround our position yet more confused, by adding to them our own ignorance. *(Applause.)*

THE CHAIRMAN: The meeting is now open for discussion. I would point out that this is a confidential meeting, and what is said here is not meant to go outside it.

MISS LAMBTON:[16] I do not feel there is very much I can add to the very able exposition of the lecturer, with which broadly speaking I agree.

There was one point which did occur to me, when he spoke of the complete religious toleration allowed by Reza Shah. That was true of the early part of his reign, but towards the end it was completely departed from and there was anything but religious toleration. Four religions were officially recognized, but there was no freedom of worship or belief at all. It was all very closely controlled, and such religious leaders as were allowed had to conform to the State doctrine.

MR. SYKES: The contention which I made, that the example of the earlier part of Reza Shah's reign is of value to Persia to-day, do you agree to that?

MISS LAMBTON: Yes, I think so.

But as regards the feeling evoked by the disappearance of Reza Shah – a disappearance for which the Persians regarded us as largely responsible – there is now great danger of a reaction because of the anarchy and chaos which has persisted in the country since his abdication; there is a danger that you will get a desire to return to that dictatorship where people at least knew where they were. At the present moment they do not.

Also, although Reza Shah went, the ruling classes have broadly speaking remained the same. They have changed from dictatorship to democracy in name. The Press and other organs of popular opinion talk about the present day as democratic but it is not at all. It is purely an aftermath of the dictatorship, and there is very grave danger that democratic or representative Government will be so discredited in the eyes of the people that they will turn away in despair to something else.

I strongly agree with what the lecturer said about Great Britain having some responsibility for fostering and furthering any movements for reform in Persia, and encouraging them and showing them what they can do in this respect.

SIR LIONEL HAWORTH:[17] As one who was in Persia through most of the period that the lecturer has been speaking about, I would like to add my agreement with the Persians in referring to the oddity of the British Government.

Persia has naturally never been able to understand Britain, and very few of us who were serving out there could do so either. With the change of party government, you get an entire change of foreign policy, and the policy is and must be naturally designed to meet the different ideas of the party in power. If you have the Conservatives, you have more or less a Conservative, i.e. a traditional Government; but when you get shall we say, a Labour Government, which believes entirely in equality and democracy, you get a reaction in foreign countries. They do not know what has happened. I as an official was saying completely the opposite from what I had been saying before, because I had to change with the Government.

I am not surprised that the Persian cannot understand us, but I do think one thing, that the study of Persian and the history of the last thirty years in Persia would make the best training for the British nation that you could possibly have. It answers in detail a great many of the points about which we are still arguing now – Imperialism, democracy, Colonial questions, giving power to the people. All these things are answered in Persia.

It seems to me impossible to imagine a completely democratic country with a people who are totally ignorant. I do not know what the present illiteracy numbers are, but the literates are very, very few. If the books were published, that the lecturer talked of, it would only be the intelligentsia who would be able to read them. You cannot in any country in the world change an autocracy into a democracy in twenty-five years. You have only one generation. It cannot be done. It is an impossibility. In a country like Persia which is a Mohammedan country it is easier, because you have the under-work, the basic system of Mohammedanism, which is democratic. The people are democratic. A man will marry a woman from any class of life. His aristocratic wife will be the top dog, but he can have wives from all different strata. I have frequently seen a man whose uncle was practically a servant. So you have a basic groundwork of democracy, but it is totally impossible that Persia to-day should be democratic.

I remember in 1906 when the Parliament was started – and as the lecturer has said, in those days they looked to us tremendously, but you cannot get away from the facts of history, and the facts of history are that Persia was a buffer state between Russia and England, and always treated as such.

It was a very convenient thing for us, for it stopped war. There is not the faintest question that there would have been war between Russia and England if there had been no Persia. But the Persian to this day regards Russia as an aggressive nation. England he has really at heart always known was not aggressive. He understood the English policy absolutely, at least all the upper classes did. For the lower class, the peasant, it simply did not come into his life, but the upper class man knew perfectly well that he was the bone between Russia and England, and as soon as England was there, he was safe from Russia. He did not believe until perhaps 1919 that England had any idea of seizing Persia.

The lecturer has mentioned to-night the 1907 treaty, which was more or less entirely a thing outside Persia and dealing with Persia. It was the Russians and English who made the treaty, but I think the 1919 treaty which we made with Persia did more to ruin our reputation than anything else in the world could have done, because that was between England and the Persian Government, and it included arrangements made by people whom the Persians thought had been bribed, arrangements by which England would really take over the charge of training the Army. Sir Percy will probably be able to correct me, I think there was also more than that with regard to the administration. I do not remember whether there was anything in the other administration, in which Sir Percy used the home Government and finance.

A MEMBER: I think any mistrust the Persians have of Great Britain dates from 1919. People ought to understand that Persia was never a country that could possibly protect itself. Reza Shah made an army of 40,000. He sent his officers to France to be trained and the army was outwardly quite a good one. But it was a totally inexperienced army, and what is 40,000 when you are talking of Russia?

But the real point of interest to us to-day is, what is going to be the outlook of the new Russia? All the time that I was there, after Imperial Russia disappeared and Soviet Russia came into being, Soviet Russia gave up things it did not want, like extra-territoriality, but you can see what Russia's real aim was in the fact that the railway that Reza Shah made from the North to the South was with one object only, to remove the dependence of Persia upon the trade of Northern Russia. That I can give you as a definite fact, because I discussed the whole matter with the power behind the throne Temar Tush,[18] who was largely responsible for it taking that direction.

At the time the British wanted the railway to run from India to Baghdad, though personally I was always in favour of the form which it took. Temar Tush discussed it very frequently with me, and he said, "The point of this is that if we can have the railway running from

North to South, we shall no longer be dependent upon Russia in any way."

It has been extraordinarily useful to us, because by a curious paradox it saved Russia. It was made against Russia, and it enabled us to send all that we had to Russia. It saved Soviet Russia.

But the thing I would like to bring out is that, when you are talking of a country like Persia, you have to have evolution in your mind. You have to see whether the thing we suggest is possible in the evolution of the country.

Also you should see that the people who direct them have been in Persia.

SIR ERNEST HOTSON: Reza Shah did his best to deprive the tribal leaders of their power. Can the lecturer tell us how far they have recovered their power?

He also did his best to prevent the migration of the tribes, and thereby upset the whole of the life of that part of the country and the economics of it. To what extent was he successful in that, and to what extent have they returned?

As to what Miss Lambton said, the Reza Shah did his best to destroy the old land-owners and tribal leaders. Who then took their place as the governing classes? Are they bureaucrats, the intelligentsia or the middle classes?

MR. SYKES: With regard to the first question, it is very difficult to give a concise reply, but I think you may generalize by saying that the Bakhtiari tribes and Khans lost their power so drastically that they have not been able to recover it. I am speaking up to about a year ago. Whether there has been any manifestation of a revival of their power since then, I do not know, but I should be very surprised to hear it.

As regards the Kashgais[19] there certainly was a very considerable revival of their activity, which started right at the end of 1941, as far as I recollect. Reza Shah's system of pacifying the Kashgais was one of the most brutal and frightful things in the whole of his reign. Statistics are very unreliable, but I have heard that as much as 45% or 50% of the population of the Kashgais tribes died, and that Persia lost 60% of the agricultural wealth of the country, that is to say in the form of their cattle and sheep and so on in the course of settling them in places where it was known they could not live all the year round. I need not remind you that they are an uneducated and very crude collection of people.

As soon as the autocracy disappeared, they rallied round their chief, the son of Sala-ud-Dowlah, and have been, as far as I know, in a state of revolt ever since.

There was violent ferment at frequent moments during the whole of the time I was there – it may have been encouraged and fostered by Germans. The Shiraz Road was closed at frequent intervals and a great many people were killed. The attempts of the Persian Army to get the better of that revolt had up to a year ago not been at all successful. In fact, they very early on had recourse to negotiations with the Khan.

As regards your, second question, I think it is addressed to Miss Lambton. I may perhaps call on her as it is a much harder one to answer.

MISS LAMBTON: The ruling classes, broadly speaking, to-day are survivors of the old land-owning families, who put their money partly into land, and the tribal leaders up to quite recently when they began to revolt, played no part.

I imagine the position of the ruling classes is very little changed since the beginning of the century, except that the religious classes play less part and the power of the big land-owners has been somewhat reduced.

But it is not a question of the middle classes or intellectuals. One of the great weaknesses of Persia is that there is no strongly organized middle class and the intellectuals are only just beginning and have very little power at the moment.

THE CHAIRMAN: I think it is time now to close. We have had a most valuable lecture. I have never listened to one from which I have learned so much.

I would first of all thank Miss Lambton, whom we may congratulate on having received the Persian award for last year for her brilliant lecture to us.

As to Mr. Christopher Sykes, I think he has dealt with this very difficult subject in the most masterly fashion.

The Reza Shah ended up a good deal like Nada [sic for Nadir] Shah. He became a most detestable tyrant. But Nadir Shah is always looked on now as a national hero, and forty years hence Reza Shah will also be looked upon as a national hero. After all, he did awfully good work at first. He modernized Persia.

Anyhow, this meeting is well justified, and we are most grateful to Mr. Christopher Sykes for what he has given us to think about.

The audience expressed their gratitude to Mr. Christopher Sykes by *prolonged applause.*

Notes

1 Christopher Sykes (1907–1986) had spent 1930–31 attached to the British Legation in Teheran. He then studied Farsi at the School of Oriental Studies, London and worked again in Teheran during the early 1940s.

2 Wilhelm Wassmuss, a German agent who encouraged Persian tribes, including the Bakhtiari, to rise up and shake off British influence. He was known as 'the German Lawrence' [of Arabia]. He died in Berlin in 1931, his exploits mainly forgotten.

3 On 31 August 1907 the Anglo-Russian Convention formalised the boundaries of control in Persia, Afghanistan and Tibet, thus marking the end of the 'Great Game'. It also put an end to the idea of Persian autonomy.

4 The Persian royal family who reigned from 1785 to 1925.

5 Dr Joseph Goebbels, Minister of Propaganda in the Nazi Government.

6 Reza Shah announced in 1935 that his country would henceforth be known as Iran, the Persian word for the land of the Aryans. It took some time for the name to be accepted, as this lecture shows. Winston Churchill continued to use the name Persia, during the war, so that 'Iran' would not be confused with 'Iraq'.

7 The Treaty, signed in Teheran on 29 January 1942, was to bring Soviet and British troops into Persia to prevent Germany from utilizing the country and its resources during the war.

8 The Treaty was preceded by a series of BBC broadcasts criticising the Shah's recent behaviour. There was close co-operation between the BBC and the Ministry of Information, and correspondence between the BBC and the Foreign Office over the line to take in its broadcasts. See 'The BBC Persian Service 1941–1979' by A. Sreberny and M. Torfel in *Historical Journal of Film Radio and Television.* 2008. Vol. 8, No. 4, pp. 515–535.

9 Mohammad Ali Foroughi, prime minister for the third time from August 1941 to March 1942. Succeeded by Ali Soheili from March 1942 to August 1942.

10 Founded in 1908, the Company had changed its name to the Anglo-Iranian Oil Company in 1935.

11 Majlis – the Lower House of the Iranian Legislature.

12 *A History of Persia,* first published in 1915.

13 The first British Council representative was appointed in 1942. The Council's priority was the teaching of English.

14 *Persia and the Persian Question* by Lord Curzon, first published in 1892.

15 *Travels in Arabia Deserta* was first published in 1888, and an abridged version was published in 1908.

16 Dr, later Professor, Ann Lambton had been the British Press Attaché in Teheran during the early part of the war.

17 Formerly Chief Political Resident in Persia 1927–1928.

18 Abdolhossein Teymourtash, Minister at Court between 1925 and 1932.

19 A nomadic tribe in south-western Persia.

Arab Nationalism Today

By Albert Hourani (1915–1993)
Lecture on 24 November 1943

Introduction

When the Ottoman Empire was partitioned up among European powers at the San Remo Conference in 1920, France got the mandate for Greater Syria. This included Lebanon, with its ancient port of Beirut, but a separate mandate was created for Lebanon, thus dividing Greater Syria into two. The Syrian National Congress attempted to install Faisal Al-Hashemi as its first king in March 1920, but the short-lived Franco-Syrian war that same year resulted in his expulsion on 24 July 1920. (Faisal was subsequently to become king of Iraq in the following year.) Both Syria and Lebanon became independent in 1943, while France itself remained under German occupation.

To the east, their neighbour Egypt been declared independent in 1922 and at the time of Hourani's lecture it was ruled by king Farouk I, a descendant of Albanian mercenaries who had served the Ottoman Empire. However, British influence continued to dominate Egypt's political life and British troops were stationed in the Suez Canal zone. Cairo was a war-time headquarters for the British as they fought Germany during the north-African campaign, until the Nazi defeat at El-Alamein in 1942.

Thus events in the Arab world were moving rapidly when Hourani delivered his lecture. Although still a comparatively young man (he was twenty-eight at the time), he had a deep and sophisticated knowledge of the Arab world. In spite of opposition to the British and French mandates which had led to armed conflict; the 'extraordinary hold' which Hitler had on the Arab imagination; the fear of Zionism; and radical 'youth movements', the lecturer found hopeful signs that Britain still had a role to play. It was not enough to have 'tutored' the emerging Arab countries before granting them a limited independence. Arab nationalists wanted help in establishing stable societies. The idea of an Arab Union was discussed, which would provide a symbol of unity, linking back to the great Arab empire of medieval times.

Britain had established in Cairo the Middle East Supply Centre (MESC), initially to meet shortages in war transport. It quickly took on a much larger role, dealing with the distribution of food supplies, the production of munitions for the army, maintaining industries, collating statistics and acting as a bureau of information. Hourani was not alone in hoping that MESC would become a joint planning organisation for Arab countries at the end of the war. (In fact it was closed down in 1945.) The lecturer believed that 'westernisation' in the Arab world would lead to a more secular society and that the British Council had a duty to spread the knowledge of English and European culture throughout this world.

PRIVATE AND CONFIDENTIAL
ROYAL CENTRAL ASIAN SOCIETY
Report of a Meeting
held at 8 Clarges Street, London W1
on November 24th, 1943
General Sir Robert Haining[1] in the Chair
Mr A. F. Hourani lecturing[2]

The main subject of my talk this afternoon will be Arab Nationalism as it was developed in the countries of the Fertile Crescent, of which I have most knowledge. I believe that a great deal of what I say applies also to the Nationalist movements in the other Arab countries, but most of my illustrations will be drawn from Syria, Lebanon, Transjordan, Palestine, and Iraq.

I lived for some years in Syria before the war, and when last year I was given the opportunity to go back once more, my main interest was to discover how the Arab Nationalists, whom I had known before the war, had changed under the impact of the war and of its events. My general conclusion would be that there has been no revolutionary change, no new ideas or new tendencies, but that the war has rather accentuated certain tendencies, which were already plain enough before it broke out.

It would be unnecessary to remind you that the whole movement of thought and of life in the Arab world in our time dates back to the sudden violent revolutionary change which was introduced into Arab life by the impact of the West in the nineteenth century. That change produced a complex and in some ways an abnormal frame of mind. Firstly, a sense of lostness, a consciousness that all one's roots were gone, that one no longer had a community which one could call one's own. The war has accentuated that. The prevailing restlessness of the world has had its effect on Arab minds. Then as another characteristic of this complicated state of mind there is the mingled attraction and revulsion which most educated Arabs feel towards the West. The Arabs have got past the stages of naïve acceptance of the whole of lestern civilization or of complete rejection of it. They have an admiration for and an interest in all the manifestations of the Western genius, but at the same time it is impossible to deny that the effect of the war has been considerably to decrease the prestige of the West among the Arabs. On the whole there has been a tendency to regard this war as a sign of a very profound malady in Europe and in Western civilisation, and to draw no distinctions inside Europe.

Another element in the state of mind is that sense of humiliation which is perhaps the most obvious and dangerous characteristic of the Arab mind in our time. The Arabs are a people dominated by their historic imagination, an imagination which has been centred almost entirely upon the glories, real or supposed, of the early Moslem centuries. On the one hand, they have this memory of past glories; on the other hand, they have a consciousness of their own weakness and impotence in the present time, and that has been increased by the events of the war. Many Arabs have said to me, "We Arabs have lived on the margin of history. At the moment when world history has come to its crisis, we have played no worthy part." That contrast between their powerlessness in the present, and the importance of their past, has produced a very dangerous sense of humiliation.

Although the war has increased the maladies of the Arab mind, it has also strengthened the will to overcome those maladies, which in its political aspect has given rise to Arab Nationalism, but which is much more than a political phenomenon.

At the same time, the war has also brought to a point the conflict of tendencies inside the Nationalist movement. As I see it, the Arab National movement is faced with a choice between two paths, which will take it in opposite directions. There are two spirits which are struggling for domination of the Arab movement. On the one hand, there is the tendency to borrow from the West nothing except its material strength, to keep aloof from the spirit of the West and to produce out of the Arab and Moslem civilization a specifically Arab and Moslem spirit. If this tendency prevails, there will be a danger of the Arab movement becoming a movement away from the West, and ultimately, I am afraid, a movement without a purpose, a movement which is essentially destructive, drawing such positive ideals as it has from a primitive Islamic social idealism.

One can remember from Arab history various movements of this sort which have prevailed in different parts of the Arab world for a time: for example the Qarmathian movement[3] and the many outbursts of Mahdism.[4]

That is one path which the Arab movement can take. The other path is that of thoroughgoing Westernization, not only in material things but also in essentials. I do not mean to say that the final destiny of the Arab people will be to become Westernized. It may be that they have something of their own to give to the world. But certainly it seems essential that as a preliminary to anything else, the Arabs should thoroughly understand and assimilate the best in European civilization. For this co-operation with the Western nations is the essential, although it must be on a footing of equality.

Those are the two main paths which the Arab movement can follow, either the path away from Europe or towards Europe.

This conflict is partly a conflict between generations, partly between different groups, different social and educational groups, but also to a great extent a conflict within the individual souls of the Nationalists. It is a conflict which is not yet decided and for that reason it is of vital importance that, whatever policy the Western Powers adopt towards the Arabs, should be such as to drive them along what I regard as the healthy path, the path of co-operation, the path towards communion with Europe.

Without entering into past controversies, it would be undeniable that the policy which has been followed in the last twenty or thirty years has tended to drive the Arabs along the path of hatred, excommunication and destruction. That goes back to the last peace settlement and especially to the expulsion of Faisal from Damascus.[5] That, I regard as the turning point in the first phase of the Arab movement. I remember when I was in Damascus, Shukri Quwatli[6] told me that he thought 'the whole spirit of the Arab movement had changed and changed for the worse on the day the French drove Faisal out of Damascus. Before that, he said, we believed in the West and wanted to co-operate, but on the day Faisal was driven out, cynicism entered in and a sort of despair.' He could not think of one person whose life and character had not in some ways been ruined by that cynicism and that despair.

Then, after the peace settlement, there came the sad history of Syria and Palestine between the wars, and finally the Iraqi revolt of 1941. If the Iraqi revolt had had even a temporary success, I do not know what might have happened. Its legend would have haunted the Arabs for years, perhaps generations. But it failed so completely that there cannot even be a legend of it: so completely that the Arab movement was forced to reconsider and to take stock of itself, and the Western powers have been given a breathing space in which they can try to help in the victory of what I regard as a progressive tendency.

There are still certain elements of danger. One of them is the extraordinary hold which the figure of Hitler has on the popular Arab imagination. I have no means of knowing how widespread this is, but certainly in the countries of the Fertile Crescent and to some extent in Egypt, a legend grew up about Hitler in the early years of the war. He was assimilated to all the heroes of early Arab and Islamic story. He was the defender, the protector. I remember, when Rommel advanced upon Egypt last year, I was told that the peasants in certain of the Egyptian villages would plot how to divide the world up among themselves. That is a trivial illustration, but it shows what a hold Hitler had over the imagination of the Arabs.

Another danger point is the genuine obsession with Zionism, the fear of it. I do not propose to enter here into the rights and wrongs of the Zionist problem, but it must be emphasized that in the Arab mind Zionism has ceased to be a problem which can be solved by certain specific particular administrative measures. It has become an all-embracing obsession which has no limits.

There is surely no need at this stage of the war to remind you what a dreadful effect anti-Semitism can have upon the minds and spirits of a nation when it saps it. The Arabs are not anti-Semites, but there is always a danger of opposition to Zionism turning into something wider and more dangerous.

A third sign of danger is the growth in certain of the Arab countries, and more particularly in Egypt, of fanatical Youth Movements, some religious, some political, of which the most important is the movement which is known as the Moslem Youth in Egypt.[7] Not very much is heard of it in this country, but it has a very considerable hold over the younger generations and particularly over the student class. The ideals of these movements, in so far as they have ideals, are based upon a very elementary belief in social justice, upon a hatred of the foreigner, even upon distrust of the indigenous Christians. So far, those movements have been confined almost entirely to Egypt, but once they start, they spread, and it would not be surprising if similar movements began to spring up in Syria and Iraq.

But apart from those signs of danger, there are also some very hopeful signs among the younger generations of Arab Nationalists. The first and most hopeful is the growth of a more profound understanding of the national problem of the Arabs. When Arab Nationalism grew up at the beginning of this century, it originated mainly among people who had been brought up in the tradition of nineteenth century Liberal Democracy, and there was a tendency to think that, if only the Arabs could achieve independence, and establish the machinery of autonomous government, their problems would be ended. The younger generation has got beyond that. It is thinking less in terms of nineteenth century Liberal Democracy and more in terms of the social democracy of our own time. It is coming to recognize that independence is not an end but a beginning, and that if the Arabs are to achieve a stable government, they must achieve a stable Society.

The whole form of Arab society, the class structure, the relationship of law and custom, the basis of social obligations and the other elements in the social structure will have to be re-shaped. (One can see a similar development taking place in the Indian national movement and in the Chinese national movement.)

It manifests itself in many ways in the Arab countries. One of the most interesting for me is the organizations which have grown up in the last few years with the object of spreading among the educated Arabs a consciousness of their social problems, and of their responsibility as educated people to do something to improve social conditions.

In Syria one has the Village Welfare Service, established by the American University of Beirut. It holds summer camps in different parts of Lebanon and Syria and even in Transjordan, at which the students of the University and other young men spend a few weeks among the peasants of the villages, study their problems and at the same time do what they can with their limited resources to fight illiteracy, to improve health conditions and so on.

In Egypt there is a similar development. There is a very interesting organization called the Ruwad, of which the dominating force is, or was, Sir Ahmad Hassanein.[8] Some years ago he got together a group of young men, who decided there was something wrong in the whole state of Egypt, and that nothing could be done until people went beyond party politics and attempted to change the way of life of the Egyptian peasant and town worker. They established a settlement in the East End of Cairo similar to Toynbee Hall. Young students spend their evenings or live there and work with the industrial workers of Cairo and attempt to arrive at a better understanding of their problems and what can be done to solve them. Similarly in Cairo there is a new school of social studies, which is trying to train social workers.

Another sign of the new interest in social problems is to be found in the growth of the Socialist and Communist movements. These movements need not perhaps be taken so seriously as some people take them; to a great extent they are nothing but an expression of the desire for change. In Syria and Lebanon the authorities have tolerated the

Social Democratic movement. It has achieved a very large number of supporters in some of the towns and more advanced country districts in Lebanon. It works there not so much through the Communist Party as through an organization called the League against Fascism and Nazism, which has been staunchly pro-Allies throughout the war.

A similar development in Palestine is the foundation of the Federation of Workers Societies in Haifa. It already has between ten and twenty thousand Arab adherents, and what is the hopful sign is that it is on extremely good terms with the Labour Department of the Government of Palestine. There is a relationship of complete trust and confidence on both sides, which is a very happy sign for the future.

A third manifestation of the social consciousness is to be found in the establishment of three very good social democratic journals in the different centres of the Arab world, – one in Cairo, one in Beirut and one in Baghdad. They are not specifically Socialist, but they try to put before their Arab readers the experience of the West in dealing with social problems, and they try to arouse a consciousness of these problems among their readers.

Another sign which I think is hopeful is that I have found among groups of young educated men in Baghdad, Beirut, Damascus and Cairo a much clearer view than used to exist of the nature of British policy and what they hope for from Great Britain. I do not say that I would agree entirely with their conception of British policy. Certainly they tend to believe that things are too easy; they tend to underrate the complexities of Great Britain's position as a world Power. They tend to forget that in forming her policy, Great Britain has to take into account not only the effect of that policy upon the Arabs but upon a dozen other forces, and movements and groups. But I give you the main lines of their view for what they are worth.

What these groups of young men say is roughly this; first of all the immediate problems which have raised feelings of fear in the Arab mind, i.e. the problems of France in Syria, and Zionism in Palestine, must be solved. But when they have been solved, Great Britain cannot rest and think she has fulfilled her duty towards the Arab world. She must then try to give the Arabs some positive and permanent interest in co-operating with her, and she can only do that by showing the Arabs that she can give them some assistance in the solution of the problems of which they are themselves aware, some assistance which they could not get from any other Power.

There is a danger, my friends continue, of a time lag in British policy. They suspect, rightly or wrongly, that the underlying conception in the minds of whoever are responsible for British policy, is of a period of tutelage, ending in the granting of self-government, and after the period of tutelage is over, there will be nothing more for Great Britain to do than to leave the Arabs alone. But, my Arab friends say, surely the experience of the last twenty or thirty years has proved that it is not enough to leave people alone in order to win their friendship. Political friendship cannot be based upon gratitude for past favours.

Also it seems clear to these Arab thinkers that Great Britain's policy requires not simply a friendly Government but also a stable Government; and since, as I have tried to explain, they now regard a stable Government as impossible, until a stable society is established, they believe it to be in Great Britain's interest to help in the establishment of that stable society.

How can Great Britain carry out this policy of giving the Arabs some permanent and positive advantage in co-operating with her? Most thinking Arabs insist that it must be done as far as possible through Arab institutions, that the 'governess principle' in foreign policy is not enough, that whatever is done must be done on a basis of perfect equality and of trust. It should be done, so far as possible, in response to needs of which the Arabs are themselves aware. Again, it should be done so far as possible through semi-official bodies of the status of the British Council or the U.K.C.C. [United Kingdom Commercial Corporation]. And it should he based upon a profound and informed study of the present situation in the Arab world.

Arabs always accuse the British Government of basing its policy more upon improvisation than upon a general conception of the development of the Arab world. The war to a certain extent has had a good effect, in so far as for one reason or another quite a number of trained sociologists and agriculturists and thinkers, have found themselves in the Arab world and have applied their thoughts to its problems. (I am thinking of people like Dr. Murray the agriculturist and Prof. Ivor Evans.) It is to be hoped that after the war first-class English thinkers and students will continue to give the Arab world their attention. But it is not enough to give the Arabs some advantage in co-operating with Great Britain. It is also necessary to make them conscious that they are receiving some advantage, i.e. it is necessary to maintain some form of propaganda organization in its best sense, not only during but after the war.

That is the general conception which the educated Arabs of the younger generation have about the nature of British policy.

I want now to take two or three of the main problems, political and social, which face the Arab Nationalists, to discuss them a little, and to indicate the sort of help which the Arab Nationalists demand from Great Britain.

Firstly, the problem of Arab unity, which is much in our minds at present. I think it is important to be clear about what the Arabs hope for from unity. In the long run they hope for an accession of economic, military and diplomatic strength. But in the short run that advantage can be exaggerated. What they want is a symbol of unity. They want to feel that they are members of a great community, which has its links with the Arab Empire of the Middle Ages. Here again the Arab historic imagination is at work, trying to resolve the present conflict between its present weakness and its past greatness.

But there is another advantage to be obtained from an elementary degree of union. In Iraq, Syria, Palestine and so on, there are tendencies – tribal, religious, racial – which are driving people apart, and which, it seems to the Arabs, cannot be resolved within the framework of the small existing States. The Kurdish problem for instance: rightly or wrongly they believe the problem would be much lessened if Iraq were included in a large unit, in which the majority of the population would be Arabs. Similarly with the Druses and Alavis in Syria.

Another advantage which Iraq and Syria hope for from Arab union is, that if union is achieved it will prevent the growth of vested interests in the maintenance of the existing smaller units. The Arabs say it is not a question of remaining where you are. Either you must move closer to union now, or inevitably you will move further away. In a way it was easier to achieve union in 1920 than now, because in the meantime a separate Lebanon Government and a separate Transjordan Government have been set up, and you have a number of interests which would lose rather than gain by the merging of these governments in a larger unit. So that some degree of union must be achieved now, if it is to be achieved at all.

But it seems clear that, if union is to be achieved, Syria and Iraq must enter it on equal terms. Iraq has had a number of years of experience of government. It has the rudiments of an army and a trained Civil Service, and it seems likely that if a union were formed now, Iraq would dominate it at first. Syria would not agree to this. They do not themselves want to dominate it, but they want a relationship of equality to be established between Damascus and Baghdad.

There is a similar problem between the Lebanese and the Syrians. There again the Lebanese insist that there must be a relation of equality.

In view of these and other difficulties, it seems to be that the immediate task is the reunion of Greater Syria and the establishment in that area of a strong, efficient Government. As between Greater Syria and Iraq, the first essential is for the establishment of certain specific common organisations.

There is a very interesting pamphlet which has recently been published by Dr. Mitrany[9] who is an extremely profound thinker upon international problems, in which he argues that the way towards world peace is not by the establishment of some impressive formal and comprehensive international organization, but by the establishment of a large number of organizations, each with a limited purpose and each growing out of the immediate needs of a certain group of countries to work together on specific problems. One can think of many such organizations which could be established between Greater Syria and Iraq. In education, for example, there is a crying need in Iraq for teachers, which could be supplied even better from Syria than from any other country. Similarly there is a need for joint agricultural organizations to decide upon the development of the Jazirah.[10]

It is at this point that Great Britain's part can come in. Under the pressure of war needs, the British Government has established in Cairo the Middle East Supply Centre, which originated from the scarcity of war transport and therefore in its early stage was essentially a restrictive agency. But there seems a possibility that in future the M.E.S.C. can become much more of a joint planning organisation for the Arab countries. That development has already started. The M.E.S.C. has already called together a number of conferences, to which representatives of the different Governments have come and which have discussed and decided various questions of common interest, such as the collection of statistics and so on. There seems no limit to the development of the M.E.S.C.

Secondly, there is the problem of the economic reconstruction of the Arab countries. That is a problem which is much too vast for me to deal with, and I do not feel myself competent, but there is one danger and one opportunity which I want to make clear.

It is obvious that the economic changes which are going to take place in the Arab countries will bring with them very far-reaching social changes. We are going to see the development of new social classes, and more particularly of an industrial urban middle class. It seems to me to be of vital importance that when these classes arise, they should not regard either the British Government or private British organizations as their enemies.

There has been a tendency in Egypt for the new Egyptian commercial and industrial firms to regard the foreign firms at their rivals. That is the underlying motive for the present movement against foreign interests which you can find in Egypt. There is to me no reason why you should have that conflict. I should like to see British firms working through subsidiaries, in which Arab capitalists owned a great share of the capital and Arab directors sitting on the Boards with British directors. One has seen that in a small way. For instance, the official French

Bank of Syria and Lebanon allots a certain very small share of its capital to Arabs. Again the Syrian Petroleum Company has one or more Syrian Directors on its Board. I think that precedent could be followed.

The end of the war offers a golden opportunity for this, because one consequence of war restrictions and of the presence of Allied troops in the Arab countries has been the accumulation of an enormous amount of capital, which has so far found no outlet for investment. If no opportunity is given to it, it will tend to be invested in real estate in the towns because that is the safest investment. But I do not think that is the most profitable way for it to be invested. That also I regard as something which Great Britain can do towards the development of Arab social life; she can provide the capitalists with alternative methods of investment.

Finally, as a third example of the sort of problem we shall have to deal with, there is the problem of Arab culture. Here it is not necessary to say very much because the British Council is already in the field, and nobody who has seen it at work in the Middle East can have anything but a profound admiration for the way in which it has started its work.

But it is not enough to leave culture for the officials of the British Council and then to forget about it. There ought to be an awareness not only among officials of the British Council but among all those responsible for British policy, an awareness firstly of how important the intellectual and the teacher are in a country at the present stage of development of the Arabs. Wherever you go, if you want to know something, you have to go to the schoolmaster. He is the best educated and most thoughtful person you will find. He also has an influence on the life of the community which is infinitely greater than the influence he can have in a country like Great Britain.

There should also be an awareness of the precise task which Great Britain can perform in the Arab world. As I see it, the first task of Arab culture in our generation is profoundly to understand and to assimilate the West. That understanding has not gone very far. There is a certain understanding of some of the later manifestations of Western culture, but what I regard as the roots of European thought – Christianity, Greek thought and so on – are not fully understood.

I believe Great Britain has a special opportunity and a special task to act as the channel through which European culture flows to the Arabs. She can do that partly because the English language is more widely known than any other language among the Arabs. People read English books, whereas few read French books and very few German or Russian or Italian. Partly too because of the special place England occupies in the world.

England is in a way both inside and outside Europe. She is therefore peculiarly competent to understand Europe and to explain it. I should regard it as an opportunity missed if the British Council were to confine itself to the spread of the knowledge of English culture and if it did not regard itself as having a duty to spread not only the English culture but the general culture of Europe as seen through English eyes.

The main way in which that can be done is through men. Wherever I went, I found Arab thinkers saying, 'Why is it that we have had Americans like Van Dyck,[11] Italians like Nallino[12] and so on, living among us and exerting an enormous influence on Arab culture, but there has been no English speaker or writer of comparable rank, who has devoted himself to the study of the problems of the Arab world?"

It may be argued that Great Britain has so many demands made upon her that she cannot find such men. I should be sorry to think so, and in any case that raises another problem. At this point, where we pass over from the problems of the Arabs to the problems of England, perhaps I had best stop. *(Applause.)*

Discussion

A MEMBER: To what extent has the American war demand and the American attitude towards the Arabs been reflected in the movement towards Arab nationalism since the war started?

MR. HOURANI: I should say that there has been a double effect. There has been a certain tendency for the Arabs to look towards America, and at the same time a certain tendency for them to be distrustful of her. She is beginning to develop economic interests of her own in the Arab countries, and people are a little apprehensive. At the same time there is still a very great fund of good will which has been heaped up for the Americans by the work of their missions, and there is still a tendency to think that, even if the other United Nations try to deny the Arabs our rights, America will look after us.

Those two tendencies are conflicting at present, but the definitive attitude of the Arabs towards America has not yet been formed.

MISS WOOD: You said what a tremendous hold Hitler had over the mind of the Arab world. What is the greater attraction, his successes or his methods?

MR. HOURANI: I do not think one can say. The popular imagination works in very capricious ways. For some reason they have seized hold of this figure and formed him into a figure of legend. Of course, his successes had a great deal to do with it. Now the legend is diminishing, but it is very difficult to kill a legend once it has been started. I think it must have been his successes, and then he served as a symbol of something.

A MEMBER: On the subject of religion, I expected Mr. Hourani would say more. It always seems to me that after thirteen centuries of thinking of themselves primarily as Moslems or Christians or Jews, it is rather difficult for the Arabs to think of themselves nationally. Is this Nationalism not largely a veneer, that underneath they think of themselves primarily as Moslems or Christians and not as Arabs?

MR. HOURANI: I think there is a tendency in that direction, but one cannot state definitively what is going to be the relation between Islam and Arab Nationalism until one knows which of the two tendencies which I distinguished will gain the mastery. If the first gains the mastery, Arab Nationalism will tend to turn into Islamism of some sort. If the second, the Westernising tendency gains ground, then I think the Arab nation will tend to adopt a more secular view of life. It will not become anti-religious, but will draw a distinction, perhaps an arbitrary distinction, between the sphere of politics and the sphere of religion. They have not that distinction between Church and State which we in Europe know; but it is inherent in Western civilization, and especially in those manifestations of it which have come to the Arabs.

A MEMBER: What is the attitude of the Arabs to the restoration of the Khalifate?

MR. HOURANI: I never found any very great interest in it. There are certain interested parties who for one reason or another would be glad to see it revived, but there is no popular movement to revive it.

A MEMBER: The King of Egypt is rather keen.

MR. HOURANI: So it is said.

A MEMBER: Arising out of that, can you say anything about the position of Egypt in relation to the Arab Nationalist movement?

MR. HOURANI: There are various things to be said about that. Firstly, there is a very genuine respect for the achievements of the Egyptians in securing their independence, in electing a Government which has a certain place in international affairs; and that is increased by the fact that Cairo is the centre of Arab culture and literature.

Further, the Arabs hope for help from the Egyptian Government in solving their own problems. The Syrians and Lebanese hope for the diplomatic support of the Egyptian Government. The Iraq Government is now obtaining a very large number of teachers from Egypt. At the same time there is a certain suspicion, a certain fear, of Egyptian Imperialism.

A MEMBER: What is the influence of Saudi-Arabia on the Arab national problem?

MR. HOURANI: I think its main influence is as a symbol. The figure of the King of Saudi-Arabia has had a profound effect on the imaginations of people, for he embodies so many of the traditional Arab virtues. In virtue of that, and also because of his friendship with Great Britain, he has been able to exercise a very great influence upon Arab politicians and Government. But I do not think anybody looks for very close union between Saudi-Arabia and the Fertile Crescent at the present time, partly because the whole structure of society is different, partly for dynastic reasons, partly because the level of development is different.

A MEMBER: I should have liked to enquire, in dealing with the question of Arab unity, how far you would extend the Arab world? Would you include North-West Africa? I should also like to corroborate from my own first hand experience the position which Egypt has even in Morocco the most civilized in many ways centre of the Arab world. Also what the lecturer said about the extraordinary bitterness felt in Damascus about the Faisal incident.

MR. HOURANI: If one is defining the Arab world, one has to include Yemen and North-West Africa. But I do not think any politician in the Fertile Crescent or in Egypt thinks it desirable to establish close relations with these at the present time. The ultimate of course is for a union that would include all the Arab speaking countries.

A MEMBER: I am glad you take that view.

MRS GREGORY: Do you think that there really is an idea in the Arabic countries that they want to raise their own standard of living, so that it would be worth British capital going there and helping them to use their own capital to raise it?

MR. HOURANI: That idea is becoming very strong indeed among the younger generation. It is largely a difference of generations. It has taken a long time to move from Gladstone liberalism to Lloyd George liberalism. Generally speaking it is only the younger generation who have this idea of the raising of the social standards. But one can see the beginnings of social discontent. It is not only a movement of intellectuals. One can find a very considerable restlessness among the peasants everywhere.

A MEMBER: An Egyptian friend of mine said to me the other day, when I was talking about the Christian Copts, "Don't speak about the Christian Copts. We are all Egyptians now."

MR. HOURANI: I think most nationalists, if that question were put to them point blank, would say, as your friend did, We are all Egyptians. But that is very largely a manner of speaking.

THE CHAIRMAN: We are most extraordinarily indebted to Mr. Hourani for his talk, and I think the value of the whole thing is really that it gives you the background. When you are dealing with a nation like the Arabs, you have to know their history, because, although history does not repeat itself, it is a good guide to the future.

The other point is the need for meeting people half-way. We are so bad about that. A question was asked about Hitler. To my mind both Hitler's and Mussolini's reputation in the Middle East was so great because of their meeting people by propaganda and letting them know that they thought them a great people, and they put it over. Our propaganda tends entirely to ignore this. That is the trouble with our propaganda in these parts. It does not say what it should.

Third, where you get a part like the Middle East and Further East you meet idealism rampant. Idealism does not settle problems. What settles problems is compromise and realism, and one idealistic problem that was settled, we are now paying for. We have to bear in mind now that we have to compromise, and the way to compromise is for the other people to understand your point of view. That is why we should be much more forthcoming and much more prepared to give our views, and not be so impromptu in our dealings with that part of the world.

Meanwhile I should like to thank our lecturer very much. He has given us furiously to think, and that is what is necessary; so much is done without thought. The Vote of Thanks was carried by acclamation, after which the meeting terminated.

Notes

1 At the outbreak of World War II Robert Haining was appointed General Officer Commanding-in-Chief Western Command and moved on to be Vice Chief of the Imperial General Staff in 1940. He was appointed Intendant General for Middle East Forces in 1941: Prime Minister Winston Churchill described the role of an Intendant General to be that of 'serving the Commander-in-Chief with the largest possible measure of supplies'. He retired from the British Army in 1942.

2 Albert Hourani (1915–1993) was born in Manchester, of Lebanese descent. He converted from Scottish Presbyterianism to the Greek Orthodox Church. He studied at Magdalen College, Oxford and during the war worked in the office of the British Minister of State in Cairo. He went on to have a distinguished academic career as an historian.

3 A radical Shi'a group, whose influence was declining by the end of the first millennium.

4 A *mahdi* is an Islamic redeemer, or someone who claims similar powers, e.g. Muhammad Ahmad bin Abd Allah (1845–1885), a religious leader of the Samaniyya order in Sudan who proclaimed himself as the Mahdi in 1881.

5 Faisal al-Hashemi was the short-lived king of Syria (March 1920–July 1920). Syria had been mandated to France in the breakup of the Ottoman Empire. Faisal subsequently became king of Iraq, which was under British mandate.

6 Appointed president of Syria on 17 August 1943.

7 This is either a reference to the Muslim Brotherhood, a conservative Sunni movement, founded in Egypt in 1928, or more likely to the para-military Young Egypt Society of the mid-1930s.

8 Ahmad Muhammad Hasanein Pasha was a senior palace official in the court of King Fuad of Egypt and subsequently King Farouk. He was an explorer and traveller, who had been a student at Oxford. He accompanied Fuad to England on a state visit in 1927.

9 Dr David Mitrany (1888–1975) historian and political theorist

10 Al-jazirah, the northern section of Mesopotamia

11 Cornelius Van Alen Van Dyck, M.D. (13 August 1818–13 November 1895) was an American missionary

12 Carlo Alfonso Nallino (18 February 1872–25 July 1938) was an Italian orientalist.

LECTURE SIX

A Forecast of Arab Unity

By Colonel S.F. Newcombe (1878–1956)[1]
Lecture in December 1943

Introduction

Colonel Newcombe's lecture was given two weeks after that by Albert Hourani (Lecture Five) and it pursues the same theme of the future of the Arab world after the end of World War Two. But where Hourani's lecture was an intellectual exploration of the Arab psyche, Newcombe's lecture is very specific about what could be done. 'General Nuri Said' who invited Newcombe to Baghdad in Autumn 1943, is Nuri al-Said, the pro-British prime minister of Iraq, who served seven terms of office and who was assassinated in the coup of 1958 that ended the Hashemite monarchy.[2] Some of al-Said's proposals were adopted and the Arab League was set up in March 1945, with founder members Syria, Lebanon, Transjordan, Egypt, Iraq, and Saudi Arabia. Yemen joined two months later.

However, at the end of 1943, it was envisaged by the lecturer as still very much a British-controlled operation. A British Minister of State and staff would be installed in Cairo, and a dedicated Department in London. The importance of communications from 'Gibraltar to the Indian Ocean' was taken for granted, as was the assumption that the Indian sub-continent would remain tied to Britain in the future, possibly with dominion status. In fact Indian independence was less than five years away.

Practical measures were discussed including help via the Middle East Supply Centre (MESC), the powerful organisation originally set up in April 1941 to control wartime shipping for the Allies (see p. 75). By the summer of 1942 it had become a joint Anglo-American body. Its remit soon included locust control, standardising medical drugs, encouraging cultivation of basic foodstuffs, improving the health of the Arab populations, development of railways, irrigation, electricity, etc. At the same time, the United Kingdom Commercial Corporation

(UKCC) was working with the Middle East Supply Centre. It had been set up in 1940 to prevent strategic goods from falling into enemy hands, and by the end of 1943 was the sole importer of many food-stuffs to the Middle East, allocating shipping, storage, distribution of goods and other essential tasks.

Oil in Saudi Arabia was beginning to be exploited by 'American interests'. Anthony Eden's Parliamentary speech favouring some Arab unity was mentioned approvingly. Jews in Palestine were to have semi-autonomy, but there is no mention of the Jewish homeland (Israel), which was established four years later.

This lecture was published in the May 1944 *Journal of Asian Affairs* with no external indication of when it was delivered. However, a tran-script of the discussion following the lecture has been found in the archives. Misleadingly a handwritten note indicates the discussion took place on 8 December 1944, though it is clear it followed imme-diately after the lecture. A revised date of 8 December 1943 would be more accurate. The discussion deals mainly with practical questions including the future role of the MESC, the provision of gumboots against bilharzia, minority communities within the proposed league, etc. There are 11 sheets of discussion starting at page 12. It is likely the original lecture transcript took up the first eleven pages.

PRIVATE AND CONFIDENTIAL
ROYAL CENTRAL ASIAN SOCIETY
Report of a Meeting
held at 8 Clarges Street, London W1
Colonel S.F. Newcombe lecturing

In the autumn I was invited by General Nuri Said to visit Baghdad as a guest of the Iraq Government to learn their point of view on Arab unity. His proposals may be summarized as follows:

1. Syria, Lebanon, Palestine and Transjordan to be reunited into one State.
2. The people of that State to decide its form of government, and whether they have a King or President as head, and whether it be one State or Federal.
3. An Arab League to be formed: Iraq and Syria to join at once. Other Arab States can join if and when they want to.
4. The Arab League to have a Permanent Council nominated by the Member States and presided over by one of the Rulers of the States, to be chosen by the States concerned.

5. The Arab Council to be responsible for: (a) Defence, (b) Foreign Affairs, (c) Currency, (d) Communications, (e) Customs, (f) Protection of Minority Rights.
6. Jews in Palestine to have semi-autonomy: their own rural and urban district administration, including schools, health and police, subject to general supervision by the Syrian State (under international guarantee).
7. Jerusalem to have a special commission of three theocratic religions to ensure free access and worship.
8. If required, Maronites in Lebanon[3] to have privileged regime.

Politically, only Iraq and a greater Syria are concerned in these proposals at present. Saudi Arabia and Egypt are not concerned as yet but are interested in other ways. It is too early to say how Arab unity will develop; the Arabs are only now exchanging views and formulating their plans, and some of their leaders in Syria and Palestine are not yet free to speak, and it is rather difficult for the people to express their views in open discussion, especially in war-time. But the outlook of the Greater Syria and Iraq is, on the whole, one of progress, education and development by their own people; like that of Ataturk, it would develop their country on modern lines with no religious interference. There are varying shades of opinion, but the principal leaders are Nuri Said in Iraq and Shukri Koweitli[4] in Syria

Nuri Said has co-operated with us since 1917. He helped with his moderation at the Palestine Conference in 1939. In August, 1940, just after the fall of France, he proposed semi-officially the entrance of Iraq into the war on the British side. If the Palestine question were settled by Great Britain on the lines of the White Paper,[5] he offered two Iraqi divisions to serve under General Wavell. He also proposed to establish an Iraqi Legation in America. His speech of December 15, 1940, which indicates the above, proves that Nuri Said supported us at our worst time and resigned from Rashid Ali's Cabinet. That speech of his is not sufficiently known. It was published in Iraq but not in this country.

Shukri Koweitli is not known in England. He is a strong, clear-minded, clear-headed character, who knows what he wants. He was voted for by 118 out of 120 delegates in Damascus, and is the only leader to count. He is a friend of Ibn Sa'ud and a devout Moslem. He said his policy was the same as in 1915, when, as a member of the Arab Nationalist Committee, he asked Emir Faisal to invite the Emir of Mecca to negotiate direct with Great Britain on "a policy of Arab freedom supported by British co-operation." That policy he still follows. Arabs, he said, need British co-operation; since 1915, and especially since Lord Curzon turned Emir Faisal over to Clemenceau in 1919,[6] Syria has had to face many difficulties; in 1941 the former policy was again renewed.

Syria has been occupied with revolution for twenty years and has made little progress compared to Iraq and Transjordan; Shukri Koweitli hopes to ensure to all Syrians equal civic rights and that general progress which has been needed for a long time; and he hopes that all Arabs without exception should collaborate cordially so as to come to an agreement on a Federal, Confederal or other basis. He realizes the need of safeguarding communications by Great Britain for general international welfare, and that Arabs should co-operate with Great Britain. The general principles of the Palestine White Paper are accepted by him and by Arabs generally, but it is for Palestine Arabs to put forward suggestions.

Bishara Khouri,[7] President of Lebanon, spoke moderately and sensibly. A Maronite lawyer, about sixty-five years of age, courteous, cultured, of simple appearance, he intends to co-operate closely with Syria and abolish needless inter-state obstacles, and had therefore elected a leading Moslem, Riad Selh,[8] a practical man, as Prime Minister. A large section of Maronites fear Arab unity, fearing that Moslems will never treat them as equals. This section would prefer a small Lebanon, in which Christians would have an 80 per cent majority. But Moslem leaders in Syria welcome the greater Lebanon, because Moslems and Christians will be in equal numbers, which will remove the fear of Christian v. Moslem and diminish the religious question in politics. The Syrians and Lebanese are determined to have independence. Their main complaint was that the French held *les intérêts communs* [the collective interests], customs, control of the frontiers, public security, administration of Bedouin; that they keep harbour dues, etc., from which they pay their own French officials, and that, in the name of public security, these *officiers des services* interfere in everything. They had to have two Budgets with divided financial control, which they do not consider is independence. (Many of these difficulties have now, been removed.)

In each of these countries naturally there are different views. Kurds in Iraq may prefer semi-autonomy, Assyrians require to be settled somewhere in safety, Druses and Ismailia in Syria may not agree with Damascus, but on the whole all require a greater Syria joined to Iraq politically as broadly outlined by Nuri Said. Whilst it is left to the people to decide on a King or President, I believe some Moslem leaders prefer the latter in order to avoid personal or family difficulties and also to reduce religious controversy; Syria and Iraq have Shia, Sunni, Druse and Ismailia Moslems, many Christian sects and Jews;

and, like Ataturk, their leaders want no religious interference with State affairs. That, however, is for them to decide. On the whole, they look to develop their countries with Western ideas of progress and education. They have vast room for expansion. Iraq now has some 3 millions where there is said to have been 25 millions before the Mongol invasion.

In Palestine and Transjordan, Arabs are believed to be much in favour of the principle of Arab unity, but the Palestine leaders are at present somewhat inarticulate. The Palestine White Paper of 1939 is accepted by practically all Arab leaders and a far greater number of Jews than is supposed are ready to come to terms on that basis. We are bound broadly on the Maugham Commission's report – i.e., White Paper 5,974. In Iraq and Greater Syria, Nuri Said's proposals are accepted almost unanimously.

As regards British interests, all Arab leaders I have seen recognize (1) that communication from Gibraltar to the Indian Ocean must be secure for British and even world commerce, (2) that they themselves require protection from outside aggression.

The Committee of Imperial Defence can best state our needs for security and can ask Arab States to co-operate by informing us of their local anxieties and contributions for defence. This principle underlies the present treaties with Egypt and Iraq, and it is assumed that Great Britain would be acting on behalf of the U.S.A., Russia and France, or other Powers.

Saudi Arabia is separated from Iraq and Syria by 500 miles of desert which is as bad as 2,000 miles of sea; Mecca and Medina are the main cities and no big schemes of development exist, except oil and gold-mining.[9] Her people are all Moslems and not divided by various religions, and there are no Christian or Jewish citizens. Saudi Arabia does not affect our communications, and it is scarcely threatened from outside.

Ibn Sa'ud has great influence, partly due to his extraordinary personality and sense, and partly because he controls the holy places. He wants no European advisers. His political outlook and interests are very different from those of Syria and Iraq, and so are our interests with him. They are mainly concerned with the Islamic world.

Egypt, too, has little political interest to-day in political unity of Iraq and Syria, but the meetings held by Nahas Pasha[10] of Arab leaders should lead to much closer co-operation in economics, research for agriculture and health, and in education and literature, as well as in political and military support.

Roughly, then, Greater Syria and Iraq want to become one political unit, as in Nuri's scheme. What form that unity takes is for them to

Nomadic
Kurds in a
summer
camp, 1928.
Copyright
RSAA.

RAF survey
plane near
Baghdad,
1934.
Copyright
RSAA.

British
surveying
party in
Iraq, 1934.
Copyright
RSAA.

Railway bridge at Ahvaz, Khuzastan, Persia, 1930s, constructed under Reza
Shah Pahlevi's modernisation programme. Copyright RSAA.

The main post and telegraph office, Teheran, under construction, 1930s.
Copyright RSAA.

ROYAL   CENTRAL   ASIAN   SOCIETY

Report of a Private Meeting
held at 8 Clarges Street, W.
on the 9th July, 1942, at 5.30 p.m.

Chairman:

Sir JOHN SHEA.

Wing-Commander J. R. A. EMBLING:

I r a q

I am speaking entirely from memory and also from a rather
restricted point of view of what happened out there.   I was
in Basra and not in Bagdad, and was concerned with a good
deal of detail work, which did not allow me to take a very
big view.

I will not go into the details of the history of Iraq
or the last twenty years with the mandate and the eventual
establishment of the kingdom of Iraq.   I would like to start
off from a point where I arrived at the end of 1938, when I
discovered that British officials and people like myself, who
were in contact with the local people, although we were

- 1 -

First page of Lecture One. Copyright RSAA.

2nd
Battalion
Assyrian
Levies, Iraq,
1925.
Copyright
RSAA.

RAF Habbaniya, Iraq. The famous sign on the Fallujah–Ramadi road.
Copyright Mike Osborne, via RAF Habbaniya Association.

say, not for us. Saudi Arabia, the Yemen and Egypt wish to remain separate political units as at present, but all are more ready than before to support each other politically and to co-operate economically.

For ourselves, our main concern is security of communications and oil for strategic reasons. We assume that the Great Powers, including France, agree to a general policy, and that their individual interests are safeguarded and in many cases their co-operation is required. Our security of communications from Gibraltar to the Indian Ocean will require certain treaties and key points. It may be possible by treaties to get close co-operation of defence without overstepping the sovereignty of these States. As Jaafar Pasha often said: "Remove your troops from Baghdad and Iraq, but don't go too far. We know that Turkey or Iran could defeat us in a day without your support."

It is accepted there will be Regional Control of Areas. We will require a Minister of State in Cairo with a staff who are known by the people and therefore have their confidence, even more important than knowing Arabs and Arabic. The fewer administrators we have and those only the best, and the more that local talent is encouraged, the better: not for the short run but for the long run. Middle East countries would all be dealt with by the Ministry of State, Cairo, and one Department in London, instead of three as at present (Foreign Office, Colonial Office and India Office). If we have one Minister dealing with all Middle East questions it will help the various States to co-operate and may later lead to their joining a future Commonwealth of independent States, united by interest of security and economics. We shall not dominate, but, as President Dodge of the Beirut American College said, Arabs will not take advice of permanent European officials, but the best influence is through such means as the British Council and the best education.

The Middle East Supply Centre, a joint Anglo-American concern, must continue for some time its present work to regulate shipping and supplies. It has the advantage of taking the widest view of economics and is not enclosed by frontiers. The Middle East Supply Centre meeting on May 8, 1943, laid down their function to plan maintenance on a wartime basis of essential food supplies, public services and facilities, mobilize economic resources of the Middle East to the best mutual advantage, and to relate all these factors to the production programmes of Great Britain and the U.S.A. and to the state of world communication. These functions can apply after the war as well as now. (1) They reduced monthly imports from 150,000 to 50,000 tons by increasing food production of the countries themselves; (2) they conserved resources by restricting consumption and preventing waste, yet ensured essential needs at fair prices; (3) they prohibited needless imports and controlled commodities in short supply; (4) they made goods locally for the armed forces.

The U.K.C.C. work with the Middle East Supply Centre in allotting shipping and the storage and distribution of pooled commodities, and

(a) Assist Government by importing bulk supplies for civil needs. The U.K.C.C. is the sole importer of cereals, rice, sugar, etc., oil, hides and fertilizers.
(b) Assist industry by importing raw materials.
(c) Place orders in Palestine for boots, tents and whatever can be made there.
(d) Allocate shipping space for essential exports from the U.K. and U.S.A.
(e) Sponsor local resources, such as production of sulphuric and other acids and of superphosphate fertilizers.
(f) Help importers re payment for imports from the United Kingdom by guarantees against transfer risks, deviation of voyages.
(g) Provide storage for stocks for 100,000 tons.

The Middle East Supply Centre co-ordinated control of locusts in five or more States; standardized medical drugs and appliances enabling medical resources to be pooled by all Middle East States; extended the growing of seed potatoes, as they had already done in Malta and Palestine, to other Middle East countries; sent the early growing of wheat of Palestine to be sown in Iraq and Iran. Three irrigation schemes have been started in Iran, another prepared for the Euphrates, and a tunnel in the Litani River made by the South African Army brings water to 7,000 acres. The Middle East Supply Centre has proved its use in war and can be invaluable to economic co-operation in peace.

A statistical conference was arranged for regular exchange of statistical data prepared on one system between Middle East countries, each having a representative on a permanent standing committee with interchange of agricultural research and data over a wide area. Programmes for education and agricultural research are being drawn up; cultivators are put into touch with research and hire tractors from a special tractor board. Like the Crown Agents, the Middle East Supply Centre can not only purchase the right goods but also get the advice of the best experts for big engineering or industrial projects.

To indicate the money available in the Near East, Palestine has £30 million instead of the prewar £6 million in circulation, and £41 million instead of £8 million pre-war in bank deposits. Iraq has some £40 million instead of £6 million currency.

Gold in terms of pre-war purchasing power: United Kingdom 12s. 6d., Egypt 8s., Palestine 6s. 8d., Iran 4s., Iraq 3s. 6d., Syria and Lebanon 3s.

1935–37	Percentage Total Exports	within Region	Percentage. Total Imports	within Region
Egypt	107.0	2.0	102.0	2.0
Palestine	13.6	11.0	48.0	15.0
Syria and Lebanon	40.0	47.0	24.4	12.0
Iraq	12.0	18.0	23.5	4.0

It must be remembered that these countries are not at present complimentary in economics. They can be very much more so. There will be vast sums in banks and currency to be spent by Middle East countries; to spend it usefully will require abnormal organization.

One of the most essential needs is improvement of health. Dr. Hoff, sent out by the U.S.A. on research, asked me to visit an Iraq village to see the people; he said 75 per cent, were diseased with malaria, dysentery, etc., and that £4,000,000 would stamp out many of these diseases. Child mortality is perhaps 60 per cent. He said we spent far too much on propaganda and too little on helping the people. Dr. Clelland, of the American University, Cairo, reported in 1937 much the same of Egypt, and said that, owing to bilharzia and other diseases, the physical strength of Saidis is half what it was thirty years ago. The Middle East Supply Centre, with America's Rockefeller Institute and existing institutions, can help in this health problem. The money is there and the problem is a serious one. Medical research could be centralized at Beirut, whereas research on agriculture for all the Middle East area might be increased in Cairo.

Transport has hitherto been organized for each small country separately, but Iraq and Syria now want to plan as one and to build a railway from Baghdad to Homs, developing the land west of Palmyra and helping the Jezira; this would be far cheaper and more economical than the Haifa to Baghdad line.

The Turkish railway to Diarbekr may be continued to Mosul, and if so the existing line, Mosul to Tel Kotchek, will be redundant. Many roads have been improved by the British troops and the broad-gauge line has been taken from Haifa to Tripoli; but improved transport is needed from Damascus to Haifa, through difficult country. Incidentally, the road, Cairo–Akaba–Jof–Koweit, has proved quite easy for motor-cars, running in Ibn Sa'ud's area some 100 miles south of the pipe line. Motor lorries and cars for disposal may be bought by the Iraq Government after the war, and they hope to co-operate with Syria in a monopolized and controlled motor traffic to and from Baghdad. Also it is proposed to take the railway from Basra to Fao, which will become the deep-sea harbour.

Irrigation and electric power, too, must be considered as a whole. It is said that Iraq could increase her population from 3½ to 25 million, and Syria from 4 to 8 million or more by irrigation. The population of Egypt, on the other hand, is about 17 million, and, as Dr. Clelland shows, it is too large for the cultivated area even after Lake Tana has been dammed.

The petty hindrances to trade and travel, both pre-war and to-day, are ludicrous. Egypt hinders the export of eggs to Palestine until the price of wheat is lowered, refuses to buy Jaffa oranges because a few oranges are grown in Egypt. Customs and barriers exist needlessly. Nothing annoyed me more than to pay nearly £1 to enter Damascus from Iraq as an entrance fee.

The Egyptian Government report (May, 1942) 1,500 square miles of surface iron ore, 200 million tons of best quality accessible; the Assuan dam will provide the required power.

Oil in Saudi Arabia is held by American interests and is said to be enormous in quantity – much more than in Iraq or Iran; this may be optimistic, but large quantities are already proved.

There is vast scope for useful work and development post-war in the Middle East area, and for improving standards, and the Middle East Supply Centre has proved the value of economic co-operation many times.

The United Nations – not Great Britain alone – will have to give the final decisions, though ours is the greatest responsibility and we have the most direct interest. We should continue, therefore, the existing Middle East Supply Centre for economics, and also the British Council's cultural and educational work, co-operate with Nuri and Shukri Koweitli at a Round Table for safety of communications, and give all Arab countries complete independence internally.

Discussion

THE CHAIRMAN: I am sure we are very deeply indebted to Col. Newcombe for his most interesting paper, and, as he said, he will now welcome your views and your questions, which I hope will be very full and many.

As, very unfortunately for me, I have to leave, I would ask your pardon for my doing so, but Sir Angus Gillan has very kindly said that he will take the Chair.

SIR ANGUS GILLAN took the Chair.

Col. Newcombe said that the general feeling amongst some of the Arab countries is that any military force that we can have in the future there should not be seen but should be somewhere in the neighbourhood. Is it possible to do that? I am thinking of our arrangement with Egypt, whereby we have a right to certain positions on the Canal and so on. Would it be possible in the re-settlement of the Middle East for whatever force there is there or outside, whether it is a United Nations force or a purely British force, to have certain positions which would not be a trouble to the morale of the Arab population and would at the same time be useful in guaranteeing communications which we must have.

COL. NEWCOMBE: We had this treaty with Eygpt in 1936, in which we were going to have all our troops in the Canal area and quite rightly. Nobody would see troops at all. It gives them the support they require, the physical and moral support. You need not after all occupy the main city provided the troops are somewhere in the neighbourhood. It is a matter of give and take. Certainly Habbaniya in Iraq causes no ill-feeling whatever, nor would the Suez Canal, being away from the main centre of government.

Then with air power, I do not think many people yet know what the garrison has really got to be. It is very much smaller now than it need have been before.

SIR PERCY SYKES: I did not catch everything our lecturer said, but I have always had the feeling that if the Jewish question could be settled, with a much bigger area, including Syria, coming into it and so on, that that would halve the trouble with the Arabs.

COL. NEWCOMBE: I have been asked to say nothing about the Palestine question. As a matter of fact there is a very good summary of suggestions in Nuri Said's Blue Book to which I have referred, but I was asked to keep Palestine as much as I could out of it.

———: Is there at present any practical suggestion how to avoid this increase of bilharzia by permanent irrigation? And is it permitted to ask whether Nuri Said expressed any views about the future of the Arabs further west in Libya and Cyrenaica?

COL. NEWCOMBE: About bilharzia I did try to find out more as to what could be done on those lines. I have no doubt they are working on it, but I really could not give you an answer because I know nothing about medical research. I do feel that by spending really large sums of money, something can be done. Dr. Hoff said, "Spend four million pounds in Iraq. You can knock out a good many of these various complaints," and I presume the same thing applies to Egypt with bilharzia.

Arab leaders leave out definitely the question of the Western Arabs at this stage on purpose. There is a sentimental, and even more than a sentimental, connection between the Western Arabs and the others, but they said, "This is all we want now. Let us get on with this." I tried to convey that here is something definite. Let us go for it and cut out these other questions that do not apply. Then we can get something done.

———: There is one very simple way of curing that bilharzia immediately. Have something done in the way of gum boots. That would prevent it. But it is difficult to get the gum boots, and to persuade them to use them.

COL. NEWCOMBE: It is difficult to pay for them too.

———: Did Nuri Said say anything about his relations with Turkey and Iran?

COL. NEWCOMBE: No, he did not mention that, but I do not think that there is anything conflicting at all. There won't be any difficulty about that, I think.

———: I was interested in the comments of Turkey after the Lebanon agreement, their fear of an unfriendly neighbour.

COL. NEWCOMBE: I know the Turkish Ambassador here very well and the former Ambassador, and as far as I can see both of them are very happy with this Arab Unity. Their general idea is that it is quite all right from their point of view, and therefore why should not [the] Saadabad pact continue?[11] But I have no real inside knowledge on that subject.

———: You spoke about something definite. That it was going to be a Greater Syria and Lebanon, with Iraq as the unit. Then the M.E.S.C. and all that, is that going to be run from Cairo? Is Egypt going to work on that?

COL. NEWCOMBE: There is no real interest in Egypt in the joining of Syria and Iraq politically. I should have divided my lecture into two parts, the first, the political part; Iraq joining Syria, which I consider is very definite indeed.

The other problem is the economic question, which is represented, I think, by the M.E.S.C. co-operating with Egypt and these other countries. It is hoped that it will continue for a few years after the war, because there will not be enough shipping: if we can get over the jealous feeling of independence of Egypt and the other countries.

———: As a temporary measure?

COL. NEWCOMBE: Yes. It should continue in my view. It must

continue for a few years. I hope it will continue permanently, because it is really of benefit to all concerned.

_____: May I ask again: is Egypt really going to welcome this new M.E. Supply Centre?

COL. NEWCOMBE: No, they are not going to welcome it if it interferes with their independence.

_____: What are the communications with Iran now?

COL. NEWCOMBE: I am not very well up in the communications with Iran.

_____: Between Iran and the Arab countries?

COL. NEWCOMBE: You have Khanikin and the Erbil-Rowanduz Road. I do not think there are any more, or that any more are projected. I have here the projects of Iraq for their new railways, and nothing new is brought in except an extension from Mosul to Erbil.

_____: With regard to the fear of other places about this union, my grandmother travelled through that part of the country in the nineties and came in touch with all the different States. Is it not true that the outside nations do not need to fear a tremendous unity, because all the little States will want their little autonomy in the bigger States. Are they going to be allowed autonomy in the federated State?

COL. NEWCOMBE: No. You have your Druses, for example, and your Maronites in Syria. But the Maronites are now in the Greater Lebanon instead of the Smaller Lebanon. They are fifty-fifty Moslems and fifty-fifty Christians. They are perfectly happy. It is only certain sections of the Maronites are still rather frightened of the Moslems' overpowering the Christians, but on the whole that has been very quickly removed. As I said, I was surprised when one of the most Moslem of Moslems said how glad they were that we had a greater Lebanon, although it was a sacrifice to Syria, because it removed that Moslem-Christian antipathy. It is no worse than our Methodists and Catholics and all our other differences of religion in this country.

H. BOWMAN: The head of the Christian community has said it is rather interesting that in the recent troubles between France and the Lebanon, the communities in the Lebanon, the Druses, the Maronites and the other smaller Christian communities, have shown an absolute and complete unity with the Moslems in their desire for independence. There has been no inter-community question at all arising. They have been combined in a way which most of us have never seen before.

I really did not rise to speak at all on that question but to ask Col. Newcombe one question on the M.E.S.C. It seems to me the M.E.S.C. might very well continue after the war, perhaps permanently. But personally I would like to see representation of the countries themselves on the M.E.S.C. At present it is entirely Anglo-American. Would it not be possible to have that M.E.S.C. on a much broader basis to have the branches in Jerusalem, Damascus, Beirut, and the Headquarters in Cairo? In that way the countries concerned would feel that they really had got a say in the matter themselves and were not being told what to do by English and Americans only.

COL. NEWCOMBE: I very strongly indeed support that. It has always been, since the M.E.S.C. started, my criticism of the M.E.S.C. that they have not brought the local people very much more on to their Boards and Committees and so on. I enquired in Cairo why it was not done, and I think a good deal of it was due to suspicion and perhaps to the not abnormal custom of the country that directly you let Mohammed or Achmed know anything, he lets his relations know first. It is one of the difficulties of control. You have to overcome that, and you have to bring these people right in and let them feel it is just as much their show as ours. Then it will succeed. If you do not let them have their fair share, it will fail.

———: The roads have been built for the people. Would it not be possible for the M.E.S.C., or whoever is responsible, to build a strategic railway. Even if the railway does go to Homs, how are you going to get over the difficulty of getting through the Lebanon?

COL. NEWCOMBE: The railway from Baghdad to Homs is a very practical line.

———: You have to go to Tripoli.

COL. NEWCOMBE: What does it matter? You have your railway built from Homs to Tripoli, and you have a line to join from Baghdad to Homs. It would cost about £3,000,000 less. It is the right line to build for the country, and who is going to pay for the strategic line? There is no more strategy necessary by going to Haifa than going to Tripoli, if the Imperial Defence Committee so organize their defence. You do want a better railway from Baghdad to the Mediterranean. It does not necessarily mean bad strategy to go to Homs and Tripoli.

———: Do you think there are enough people behind Shukri Koweitli and Nuri to carry on, if anything happened to them?

COL. NEWCOMBE: If you give people a certain amount of responsibility and a job to do, I do not know that they make more mistakes than we do. We make them in different directions. We make them in one way and they in another.

———: On the economic side some years ago a friend of mine was asked by Nahas Pasha to go round Iraq and give his recommendations on getting capital into the country. The Iraq Government gave him all facilities for seeing the place. When he got back, he said: "Quite frankly, I am not going to recommend anybody to put anything in this country for the reason you have not got the people to work it. You have no labour. Until you get your child mortality down and your population up, you will never get any capital into the country." Do you confirm that, or does that apply to a certain extent to Syria as well.

COL. NEWCOMBE: I do not know whether it applies to Syria. Dr. Hoff told me the infant mortality in Iraq was 60%. It is true that the labour question would be one of the most serious. Surely, does it not depend a great deal on what you are putting your capital in? If you are putting it into irrigation, obviously you have to balance your labour up against the money you are spending; otherwise you are irrigating more land than you can use. You could, of course, import temporarily people from Egypt. They come for a year at a time, the same as they go up to the Soudan. You have also, as you know, the tribes; 15% of them now are settled down from being Bedouins to being peasants and so on. So that you have at least that Bedouin population, who are ready to sit down and work, which would develop your irrigation. It depends on what scheme you are putting up.

_____: My friend's recommendation was that you must have a balanced industry; i.e. you must have various industries and not concentrate on one. For instance, you can grow cotton there, but he was against having enormous areas under cotton and leaving the dates out of the question,

COL. NEWCOMBE: It is a complex question. Each project has to be balanced upon its merits.

MR SLATER: Colonel Newcombe has given us the most inspiring vision of the possibilities that may result from the unified and concerted action in the Middle East in such matters as health and agricultural development, agriculture and transport, and generally in material development of all kinds. He has, if I may presume to say so, laid very great and right emphasis on the important part which is now being played by the M.E.S.C. I think that that is the line on which unification of those areas is likely to have the most fruitful results, but I would like to ask a question or to put a point which gives me a certain doubt and hesitation as regards the topic before us this afternoon, and that is what advantages will arise from these projects of political combination which are put forward?

The unified and concerted action which has been described, and which is obviously of the greatest potential value, is of an economic and material character, and, another feature, it is being worked very largely at present by an extraneous or foreign agency. Is it reasonable to suppose that if these States did turn their attention now to the most complicated questions of political combination, it would not only endanger perhaps the beneficent activities of these external agencies who are now engaged in the development of the country, but might by the mere preoccupation put a stop to all such beneficent activity whilst the States were chasing this difficult illusion of federation round and round Arabia? Would it not be better for them at this stage to concentrate their efforts on taking a larger active part in these matters of material and economic development and leave the political will-o'-the-wisp alone?

COL. NEWCOMBE: I do not agree at all. You have Shukri Koweitli very definitely established in Syria and Bishara Khouri in the Lebanon. They are quite equal to carrying on themselves in those countries, provided they have not to worry about external aggression.

MR SLATER: I did not make myself quite clear. I did not refer to their internal politics but to the combination.

COL. NEWCOMBE: The main combination after all is Greater Syria, i.e. existing Syria, the Lebanon, Palestine and Transjordan. But assuming for a moment that Palestine is settled, you have four minor States which can carry on just as they are internally, with a central Federation – like you have in Australia – for deciding on the big questions.

MR SLATER: And Iraq, that is different.

COL. NEWCOMBE: I do not see it. Saudi Arabia is out of it, and Egypt, and all the Persian Gulf people. . So it is just that little group, and I do not see any vast difficulty about it. When it comes to the economic question of other States joining in – as they should do, I think – it is rather difficult in war-time. Post-war I do not see why they should not join up in the economic sense. That is the sort of thing that occurs. It does not take everybody in the country twenty-four hours a day to co-operate and join in with the Supply Centre. They gradually join up and take over their share and operate. I personally see no great difficulty about it. It is obviously a thing you do not do in a minute. You have to have a programme to get on to.

MR N. BARBOUR:[12] In listening to the address, what struck me was how very refreshing it was to have the thing on a practical basis of economic and hygienic and other development instead of being concerned entirely with politics. I asked myself why this was. I think there are two reasons. One that because of the war and the establishment of M.E.S.C. the whole unit has been treated as one for the first time. Secondly, since Mr. Eden's declaration favouring some Arab unity, Arabs have been much more willing to consider the thing as a whole; and after all the basis of the claim for Arab unity was that this country ought to be one, that if you broke it up you could never make anything of it. Since Mr. Eden's declaration, they do feel that there is a prospect of that; that there is a more sympathetic attitude on our part towards it; and they are more willing to cooperate with the

M.E.S.C. and so on. And that struck me as being such a happy thing in the talk to-day. I interpreted it exactly the reverse way to the last speaker.

THE CHAIRMAN: It only remains to me as part-time Chairman to thank Colonel Newcombe very much indeed on your behalf for his address. I do not feel really that I am qualified to sum up. My view of these Arab countries has been from a rather detached standpoint; it is true from an Arab country, but one on the other side of the Red Sea. But one naturally has always taken a great interest in that question.

I personally am most indebted to Colonel Newcombe for his address to-day. He has put the whole thing on a realistic and practical basis. Some of us have been inclined to speak rather glibly about Arab centrifugal tendencies, and look on these federal ideas as all very pretty but not quite practical politics. We have to revise these ideas.

Mr. Eden's declaration has officially committed the Government to some extent and I think it is up to us all to show by our sympathy that we are prepared to give a practical interpretation to these undertakings.

Colonel Newcombe, of course, has been at some disadvantage in having to leave out almost the Prince of Denmark but that is inevitable. But within these limits, I think he has shown us that there are practical possibilities in this limited federation.

As regards remoter prospects, I feel that possibly this M.E.S.C., if it could be developed on the lines suggested by Mr. Bowman, may provide the germ of some sort of organization which might lead on practical lines to a bigger federation in the future. But that is a thing which we need not concern ourselves with at present. The practical immediate steps are all we need worry about just now, and I do feel that in a Society of this sort, it is up to us to show our sympathy with these Arab aspirations.

On your behalf I should like to thank Colonel Newcombe very much indeed for his most intensely interesting address.

The Vote of Thanks having been carried by acclamation, the Chairman declared the meeting closed.

Notes

1 Lt Colonel Stewart Francis Newcombe led an adventurous life and was a friend of T.E. Lawrence. He served with the Egyptian Army from 1901 to 1911, and subsequently surveyed the Sinai peninsula with him. He played a key role in the British-inspired Arab revolt of 1917. Taken prisoner by the Turks, he escaped with the help of his future wife, Elizabeth Chaki. He finished his career in Malta as chief engineer, and retired in 1932 .

2 The title 'general' may be honorary, al-Said does not seem to have served as an army officer.

3 The Maronites are a Christian group of Syrian origin, founded in the 5th century AD.

4 Shukri al-Quwatli (1891–1967) was the President of Syria from 1943 to 1949 and from 1955 to 1958.

5 The White Paper of 1939, which was passed by Parliament, proposed an independent Palestine governed by Palestinian Arabs and Jews in proportion to their numbers in 1939. Restrictions were put on the number of Jewish immigrants. The White Paper was fiercely opposed by both Jews and Arabs, but not rescinded until 1948.

6 The Sykes–Picot Agreement of 1919 divided up the Arab countries formerly part of the Ottoman Empire (excluding the Arabian peninsula), between Britain and France.

7 Bechara El Khoury (1890–1964), first post-Independence President of Lebanon, from September 1943.

8 Riad Al Solh, first post-independence prime minister of Lebanon.

9 This paper was given before the Americans had announced their projected oil pipe-line. (footnote in text – Ed.)

10 Mustafa el-Nahhas Pasha, prime minister of Egypt.

11 A non-aggression pact signed between Turkey, Iraq, Iran and Afghanistan in 1937.

12 Noel Barber, foreign correspondent for the *Daily Mail*, journalist and novelist.

The Assyrian Cause

By Air Vice-Marshall Hugh Champion de Crespignyder
c. January 1964

Introduction

The period of the British mandate in Iraq, from 1920 to 1932, saw a number of armed uprisings which were put down by ground and air troops. The lecturer notes the agreement at the Cairo conference of 1921 that Iraq was to be controlled by the Royal Air Force, rather than the army. This had been suggested by Hugh Trenchard, Marshal of the Royal Air Force, to Winston Churchill, then Colonial Secretary. It was a radical idea. The Royal Air Force had been founded only three years earlier, at the end of World War One, but had already assisted in putting down a short-lived revolt in Somaliland. In theory the RAF was to patrol difficult or inaccessible areas of deserts and mountains, thus saving the deployment of British soldiers. In practice it got off to a shaky start. Bombing raids were carried out, particularly over Kurdish areas, in an effort to persuade the tribes to cease their opposition to the British mandate. Although this caused fear and panic, it also strengthened local opposition.

Two RAF bases were established – the larger at Habbaniya, near Baghdad, and a smaller one at Shaibah, near Basra. Later four more bases were set up. Ground troops were required to guard the bases, and these were provided by the Assyrian Levies, who had previously been part of the Iraq Levies, formed to protect refugee camps in the chaotic break-up of the Ottoman Empire. The Assyrians, a Christian minority in a Muslim country, quickly identified themselves with the British. This made them unpopular with the Iraqis and constant friction led to an Assyrian massacre in 1933. The search for a permanent homeland outside Iraq for the Assyrians began, but in a half-hearted manner.

When Rashid Ali's pro-German assault on RAF Habbaniya took place in May 1941, the Assyrian Levies staunchly defended the base against the Iraq Army, which made their position in Iraq even more difficult. They were now renamed the Royal Air Force Levies and a rapid recruitment exercise began of compulsory 'volunteering' for civilian and military duties. About 10,000 Assyrians were in service in 1943, in the expectation that the British would remain their 'guardians'. However, when the immediate crisis was over, the levies were stepped down and the search for a permanent homeland was taken up again.

PRIVATE AND CONFIDENTIAL
ROYAL CENTRAL ASIAN SOCIETY
Report of a Meeting
held at 8 Clarges Street, London W1
Air Vice-Marshall Hugh Champion de Crespigny lecturing[1]

The Assyrian Cause
The Assyrians[2] and our obligation to them

During the present war I have for a period served among the Assyrian people and been in close personal contact with them, a people whose history goes back to thousands of years before the birth of Christ, and who at one time held a position of great power throughout the Middle East. Broken by their campaigns which culminated with the utter destruction of their ancient capital of Nineveh in 612 BC, they still exist as a small Christian minority in the north of Iraq and its neighbouring countries. Indeed, the majority still adhere to the Nestorian Church which from the sixth century AD onwards had perhaps the greatest record of any Christian Church for its missionary activities, extending its influence throughout China, India, Middle East countries, and Eastern Europe. Little has been heard of the Assyrians by the general public for some years. Some may remember that they rendered valuable services to Great Britain and her allies during the last war.[3] In the period between the two wars they were primarily responsible for safe guarding our air fields in Iraq and for providing the ground forces which are an essential complement to air control. Not only did air control in Iraq save this country many millions of pounds but it served as a model which was extended to several parts of the Empire. What is not generally appreciated is that, after severe disillusionment during that period, the services of the Assyrians to Great Britain during the present war have exceeded anything they did before. Had it not been for their loyalty at the time of Rashid Ali's German inspired revolution in Iraq[4] in May 1941 our position in the Middle East might have become most precarious. The many who have served in Iraq and met and grew to like and admire the Assyrians there will hope that amidst the problems of post war settlement we shall not overlook our obligations to them or fail to seek and to secure a solution to their unhappy situation. We have a moral responsibility to do so, for these people have been staunch friends to Great Britain for the last 28 years. They regard themselves almost as British Nationals, realising as they do that their only hope of future existence as a race depends upon our guardianship.

Their Origin and History

If doubt exists about the origin of the Assyrians there is no sound reason to disbelieve that they are descended from their namesakes who 'came down like a wolf on the fold' and had their capital at Nineveh near Mosul. The existing community represent the remnants of the Church of the East, which began to decline with the rise of Islam when large numbers of its adherents apostatized. It was further weakened by massacres at the time of the Mongol invasions and the ravages of Timur the Lame about 1400 AD. By this time the majority of the survivors had fled from the plains to the high mountains of Hakkiari in North West Kurdistan, and though in due course many of them returned to the plains, it was this district which then became the real homeland of the Assyrian people. In the sixteenth century there arose a dispute over the succession of the Patriarch, one of the rival candidates submitting to Rome. His followers came to be known as Chaldean Uniats, and now form the Chaldean Church with its Headquarters in Mosul. At the outbreak of the Great War in 1914 one group was living round Lake Urmia in Persia and another as Turkish subjects in the Hakkiari mountains. The latter were granted a considerable degree of autonomy under their religious and temporal head the Mar Shimoon[5] and they were exempt from conscription in the Turkish Army. Nevertheless, they were never happy as a Christian community living in subjection to a Moslem power. A hardy mountain people they have retained to a marked extent many of the facial characteristics of the ancient Assyrians. This martial strain combines with a certain streak of vanity and a realistic pride in their physical prowess to make them excellent material as soldiers, as their past record has already proved.

The Great War

The Great War of 1914–18 was catastrophic for the Assyrian people. Not only were their numbers ravaged by massacre and sickness but they lost their homes and their all. On 3 August, 1914, Mar Shimoon, the Patriarch, was summoned to Van by the Turkish Vali[6] and asked for an assurance that his people would not assist the Russians on whom the Turks were about to declare war. Mar Shimoon replied that the attitude of the Assyrians would depend on the Turkish treatment of the Christians of the Ottoman Empire. As soon as war was declared, the Turkish garrisons in the Hakkiari district were withdrawn, and the province was left to the tender mercies of the marauding Kurds.

The resulting disorders, plundering and murders went on throughout the winter of 1914/15 and on 12 April 1915, after a five days' conference the Assyrian leaders decided to send a declaration to the Vali of Van to the effect that owing to the massacres and oppressions to which the rayah[7] Assyrians had been subjected the six free districts felt obliged to sever their relations with the Ottoman Government and come to an understanding with the Russians and their allies. They then sent an envoy to Persia to ask for Russian help but he arrived just as the Russian commander was in the act of withdrawing his forces from Salmas, and they were left to their fate. They held out in their mountains for six months, and when food and ammunition began to run short, fought their way out to the Persian plains. There they were organised into irregular bands under Russian officers and fought for the next two years.

When the Russian revolution broke out in 1917 the Assyrians were again deserted, but they received promises of help from the British and fought on. In July 1918, the Turks drove them out of Urmia and after incredible hardships they made their way to Hamadan whence they were evacuated to a refugee camp at Baquba near Baghdad. The evacuation was not completed without further loss; the Moslems pursued the refugees, killing women and children, old and sick, and following along the road to cut the throats of the stragglers. Thousands died on the trek from starvation and exhaustion, and many from disease. Eventually the remnants, some 50,000 strong, arrived at Hamadan in the middle of August 1918. The British authorities then took them in hand and established the unique refugee camp at Baquba on the Diala river.

Plans for re-settlement

In 1920 shortly before the outbreak of the Iraq rebellion the Assyrians were moved from Baquba to Mindan in the Mosul province pending arrangements for their repatriation. It had been decided that the Urmia refugees should be the first to be repatriated returning home via Kifra and Altun Kupri, but on the advice of H.B.M.'s Minister[8] at Teheran, the scheme was abandoned owing to the disturbed state of Azerbaijan and the risk involved. The Urmia Assyrians from the outset had petitioned for a British Protectorate over them. With regard to the refugees from Turkey, it had been decided in November 1918, that the Civil Commissioner in Baghdad should approach the Foreign Office with a view to obtaining sanction to set aside as a reservation for the mountain Assyrians a certain tract of country south of Amadia and in the Mosul vilayet.[9] Later it was agreed that it would be unsafe to repatriate Christians into the midst of Kurdish tribes unless the Turks were first expelled and strong gendarmerie garrisons, including the Assyrian Battalion which had been formed at Baquba, placed at strategic points in Kurdistan. The scheme although approved did not materialise as it was considered impossible to exercise military control in the area. For some years there were various plans put forward to settle the people in an enclave under British protection somewhere in the East, and other plans to move them to Brazil, Canada or British Guiana, but these suggestions all fell through. In the meantime many obtained employment in the towns whilst others settled amongst the Kurds north of Mosul.

Formation of Assyrian Levies

At the time of the Arab revolt in Iraq in 1920, two battalions of Assyrians were formed for the defence of the refugee camps and became part of the Iraq Levies, a mixed force of Arabs, Turcomans and Kurds, 5,000 strong. In 1921 the Cairo Conference decided that the Royal Air Force should assume control of Iraq instead of the army. As Iraq was in future to have its own army, it was decided that no more Arabs should be enlisted in the Levies, and so by 1924, that force consisted of about half Assyrians and half Kurds with one company of marsh Arabs. During the next few years the strength of the Levies was steadily reduced and the proportion of Assyrians employed in it rose. They acquitted themselves well on a number of occasions on active operations against Sheikh Mahmud[10] and others. Under the terms of the Anglo Iraqi Treaty, which was drawn up in 1930, the

Levies were to be reduced to a strength of 1,250. They were to have British officers and be entirely at the disposal of the Air Officer Commanding but were to form part of the forces of H.M. the King of Iraq. This was not disclosed at the time and when it became known the Assyrians were dismayed at the prospect of again becoming subjects of a Moslem power. Like many others they had never believed that Britain really intended to surrender her mandate. They decided to assemble the whole nation in the Amadia district presumably with the idea of collective bargaining with the Iraqi authorities.

A very difficult situation was created. The Iraqi authorities were naturally perturbed at the idea of a strong force of trained soldiers antagonistic to themselves being allowed to collect in one part of their territory. Moreover, the Assyrian officers of the Levies asked to be allowed to resign their commissions within 30 days and their lead was followed by the men. This would have left our airfields unprotected and so a British battalion was flown over from Egypt.[11] The Mar Shimoon used his influence to counter this hasty decision of his people and the trouble blew over in a few days, and it became possible to send the British battalion back. This was the only occasion when there was any friction between us and the Assyrians and was entirely due to their fear of losing British protection.

The Simel massacre

In 1933 the Levies had been reduced to five Assyrian companies and one Kurdish company, with two Arab companies for service in the Basrah area which was considered climatically unsuitable for men from the hills. Although there had been no open breach with the Iraq authorities there had been constant friction and the Assyrians had never become reconciled to the prospect of becoming Iraqi subjects and were always seeking for some place where they could settle in greater security. In the summer of 1933 a party of Assyrian men crossed into Syria in the hope of finding some district there in which they could settle with their families. On their return to Iraq they were met by a detachment of the Iraqi army which had been given orders to disarm them. An action took place in which there were a number of casualties on each side. This occurrence in itself was unfortunate enough but the sequel was far worse. The Iraqi army was turned loose on the defenceless villagers who had been left behind when their menfolk had gone to Syria and there was wholesale massacre.

Such a storm of indignation arose in Europe when the facts became known that it appeared likely that the treaty[12] would have to be abrogated and the mandate resumed. That would, however, have been such a blow to Iraqi amour propre that it would almost certainly have been followed by widespread revolt throughout the county. It was decided that some home for the Assyrians must be found outside the country. Several parts of the world were inspected including Brazil, British Guiana, and Canada, but without result and the only practical measure taken was to settle a number of families on the Khabour river in Syria.

For the next ten years the Assyrians, in spite of their disappointment at having to remain Iraqi subjects remained perfectly loyal to the British, and their menfolk continued to protect the airfields of the Royal Air Force. It had originally been proposed that the Levies should be embodied in the Iraq army but no settlement had been reached by the time the present war broke out. In 1939 the force comprised H.Q. and four Assyrian companies with one company of Kurds and one of Arabs to protect the base at Habbaniya and one company of Arabs at Shaibah near Basrah. In the following year one of the Arab companies disbanded and was replaced by an Assyrian company.

Rashid Ali's revolt

This was the situation in May 1941, when the revolt organised by Rashid Ali and the Germans broke out and the Iraq army marched against the Royal Air Force base at Habbaniya. The Levies remained staunch and distinguished themselves in the fighting there, and the roundup of the Iraq army at Fellujah. It is not proposed here to go into any detail regarding this revolt which has been fully covered in other papers. Suffice it to say that although our Assyrian Levies played a considerable part in clearing up a dangerous situation, the fact that we used them against the Arab army made them still more unpopular with the Iraqis and the feeling between the two peoples degenerated into acute dislike and distrust. As on other occasions the Assyrian position vis a vis their Moslem neighbours was rendered more difficult still through their whole-hearted support of the British.

Expansion of the Levies

In the Spring of 1942 when the Axis threat to Northern Persia through the Caucasus and to Syria and Northern Iraq through Turkey began to develop seriously, it became increasingly necessary to conserve British army troops by every means within our power, in order to increase our striking forces in the forward areas. It is well known that with our heavy commitments in North Africa our total resources in the Middle East were at this time strained to the limit and any substitution [which] could be effected by locally enlisted troops to take over the more static roles would have the direct effect of increasing our front-line strength. A policy of greatly expanding the Levy force (now known as the Royal Air Force Levies) was decided upon and it was agreed that the Royal Air Force in Iraq and Persia should, as far as was possible, relieve the army from its responsibilities for guarding airfields and Air Force bases and installations. An intensive recruiting campaign was commenced, aiming at raising the strength of the force to 11,000 troops, preference being given to Assyrians on account of their proved reliability and fighting qualities. The commitments of the Air Force command had by now considerably increased and covered large areas in Persia and the south coast of the Persian Gulf. Climatically unsuitable for Assyrians the majority of the RAF Levy Companies in the Gulf area were to be locally enlisted Arabs and Baluchis, but more than half the total force was to consist of Assyrians. This meant that every able-bodied male Assyrian between the ages of 18 and 45 would be required to volunteer for service with the British. There were already approximately 5,000 serving as civilians in both the army and Air Force. In a period of just over one year the force was increased to 8,000 Air Force soldiers, nearly 5,000 of whom were Assyrians. To use the words of their own leaders with whom this vast expansion had been discussed by me 'We have nothing to give but our men and Great Britain can have them all as our only hope of future existence as a race depends upon her guardianship.'

When the Russian successes in the north removed the threat to Persia further expansion of the levies was stopped and that part of the force which became redundant to the requirement of Iraq and Persian command took over various responsibilities from the Army in other neighbouring countries. But the saving in British manpower remained the same and proportionately increased the striking power of our army. It would not be an over-estimation to state that the Assyrian race in Iraq and Eastern Syria have saved us 10,000 British nationals.

Post-War Settlement

It has sometimes been said that the Assyrians are a difficult people but I refuse to subscribe to this phrase. Their difficulties have been brought upon them throughout their recent history by their whole-hearted support of Great Britain and her allies, and they are faced now with the overwhelming problem of their existence in the future should we withdraw our influence from Iraq.

They are as a race just commencing to emerge from the tribal state and are not so accustomed as some European races to suppressing their feelings. They dislike the Arabs and indeed they have every reason to do so, and the Kurds in Northern Iraq, though closely akin to them, are their traditional enemies.

Apart from their religion the strongest trait of the Assyrians is their friendship for and loyalty to ourselves. The problem of post-war settlement in the Middle East will be [a] little less difficult than those in Europe but it is clear that the Assyrian people are never likely to settle down as peaceful subjects of an Iraqi government unless that peace is maintained from outside. They were unpopular with the people of Iraq before Rashid Ali's revolt and the large part they played in the discomfiture of the Iraq army at that time will no doubt rankle for years.

Plans to settle them in some other country where they would have reasonable hope for security have already been mentioned. Before I left Iraq, some of their leaders opened again the question of their migration to Canada and stated that since the discussions had first taken place on this proposal they had changed their minds, and a large section of them would now be only too anxious to go. Their chief desire is to settle somewhere under British protection and in view of their past and present services to this country, it would not only be unkind but immoral to disregard their wishes.

During the last two years, four other suggestions were put forward all of which have fallen through for one reason or another, but the last of which in my opinion, still holds out considerable promise.

(a) To establish a colony in Cyrenaica.[13] It was found on investigation that the total area here was not sufficient to absorb the population required, and also there are strong political objections locally.

(b) To form a colony in Northern Eritrea. An investigation was made on the spot of the country extending from Asmara to the north of Eritrea, but it was decided that the amount of money necessary for water conservation and terracing in this mountainous and arid region rendered it quite out of the question. Even after an expenditure of many millions of pounds it would never be possible to absorb the number required and the ultimate prospect would be little more than eking out a bare existence under the greatest of hardships and amongst unfriendly neighbours, The country is also climatically unsuitable for the Assyrian people and there is no doubt they would deteriorate were they to be settled in this area. Although the southern half of Eritrea provides better country, it is at present saturated with its own Ethiopian population, and too much infiltration here would cause considerable unrest.

(c) To establish a colony with a high degree of autonomy in all matters appertaining to their internal affairs on the east side of the Tigris between Samarra and the Lesser Zab, a proposal emanating from a senior member of the Iraqi government. It is the intention of the government of Iraq to develop this area agriculturally by opening up the ancient canal system, and the proposal sounded attractive. The offer has however since been denied and it would appear that no solution to the problem is to be found within the borders of the present Iraq state.

(d) To extend the present settlement on the Khabour river in eastern Syria. This area is already partially irrigated but schemes exist for making two more canals which would bring a very much larger area under irrigation. It was estimated that by the expenditure of approximately one million pounds on irrigation works, the Khabour could be so developed as to make it possible to absorb all the Assyrians with whom we are concerned, with first class prospects of establishing good farms with available markets for their produce. This scheme was abandoned owing, it is understood partly to French and partly to Syrian objections. There is little doubt that pressure would have to be brought to bear upon the Syrian Government to obtain their acceptance of this scheme and that the pan-Arab movement will cause additional difficulties.

Whatever scheme may be thought best and found most practicable, this brave and historic people must receive the guidance, encouragement and active help from Great Britain which their loyalty and gallant assistance to her during the last 28 years alike deserve. Indeed it is in keeping with the highest Christian principles and the ultimate object for which we are fighting this war that we should keep always in mind the security and future well being of the smaller and more defenceless races, especially those who have lost so much in the cause of freedom.

Notes

1 Hugh Vivian Champion de Crespigny (1897–1969) was born in Melbourne, Australia and joined the Special Reserve Royal Flying Corps during World War One. He was awarded the Distinguished Flying Cross and the Military Cross for actions in Europe during the war. He

commanded the British air forces in Iraq in World War Two and retired at the end of the war to South Africa.

2   Assyrians are descended from tribes originating in Mesopotamia in pre-historic times c. 4000 BC. During the Ottoman Empire they lived in what is today Iraq, Syria, Iran, Turkey and Lebanon. The term 'Syrian' derives from the name of the ancient kingdom of Assyria, although Assyrians and Syrians are ethnically separate today.

3   I.e. The Great War of 1914–1918.

4   See Lecture One 'Iraq 1942'.

5   Mar Shimoon, the title of the Patriach of the Church of the East.

6   *Vali* – governor.

7   *Rayah*, people subject to civil law, not clan or tribal law.

8   HBM – His Britannic Majesty's Minister.

9   *Vilayet* – province.

10 Sheikh Mahmud (1878–1956) leader of the Kurdish uprising against the British mandate.

11 Two platoons of the 1ˢᵗ Battalion Royal Inniskilling Fusiliers.

12 The Anglo-Iraqi Treaty of 1930 followed two years later by the granting of independence to Iraq.

13 Cyrenaica – the eastern coastal region of Libya.

LECTURE EIGHT

Moscow
July and August 1941

By Colonel Guy Symonds, DSO

Introduction

Shortly before the lecturer's arrival in Moscow, Germany had invaded the Soviet Union, launching Operation Barbarossa on 22 June. Both countries had signed a non-aggression treaty at the beginning of World War Two, but by 1941 this had fallen apart. Adolf Hitler had been warned by his own officials that there would be disadvantages to the invasion, not necessarily military, but the Nazi leader ignored them. The Wehrmacht (the combined German army, navy and air-force) had under-estimated Russia's military and economic strength. Germany's success in Europe, with the fall of France in June 1940 had made it over-confident. Hitler himself predicted that Russia would collapse within three months of the German occupation. At first the Nazis seemed successful, but met stiffer resistance than anticipated. The capture of Moscow, the capital, was postponed, which gave Muscovites time to prepare by digging rings of trenches around the city.

Symonds was Fire Advisor to the Home Office at the time of his visit. He had been chief officer for the fire brigade of the Durham & Northumberland Colliery Owners' Association and had previously visited Russia in 1911, before the Revolution. His brief was to see how Moscow was preparing for bombing raids, something London had been experiencing since September 1940. Although Symonds was in Russia at a crucial period of World War Two, he says nothing about the German advance and confines himself to general remarks about the war and a lot of domestic detail, which makes this account so interesting. Symonds explains that as a civil servant he was circumscribed by what he could and could not say, and had had to sign an undertaking before he could give this lecture to the Royal Central Asian

Society. Even then, his audience were strictly warned that what Symonds said was 'absolutely confidential'.

The lecturer may have been unaware of details of the German advance. Both the Nazis and the Soviets controlled the media, which consisted at the time of newspapers, radio broadcasts and newsreels. (Media control was not of course limited to the Axis powers and the Soviet Union during the war.) He could not speak Russian and therefore could not pick up on rumours. Nevertheless, he does seem, like some other Britons including the writer George Bernard Shaw, to have returned to England full of praise for the Soviet way of life: 'I have come back with a most wonderful admiration and no one has stressed the marvellous things they have done, the marvellous planning and discipline, brutal and ruthless but quite marvellous.' He found it quite reasonable that Russians were shot if they missed their fire-watching duties.

The planned German capture of the Russian capital was fiercely opposed by Muscovites. Because the Nazis thought the Soviet Union would have surrendered long before the start of the winter, its army had not been provided with winter clothing or equipment and was forced to stop its offensive at the beginning of December 1941.

PRIVATE AND CONFIDENTIAL
ROYAL CENTRAL ASIAN SOCIETY
Report of a Meeting
held at 8 Clarges Street, London W1
on Wednesday, November 26th, 1941

THE CHAIRMAN: We are very privileged to-day in having here Colonel Symonds who has been kind enough to consent to tell us about his visit to Russia. Will you please remember that this lecture is absolutely confidential. It is a most extreme and special privilege that we are allowed to have. There is a very honourable tradition in this Society that when a confidential lecture is given nothing is communicated to the Press and it is not discussed outside this room. I would remind you of that very honourable tradition with absolute and complete confidence.

COLONEL SYMONDS: First of all, I ought to apologise to the Secretary for the awful tomfoolery that has gone on about this talk. I am a Civil Servant, although a temporary one, and when one talks to anyone you have to sign statements that you will not say this or that and will not be reported. Whether it is a guilty conscience I do not know.

Secondly, I want to apologise as I see that your Secretary has put up a map of Russia. I want to apologise because I have not seen Russia. I have seen Moscow and Archangel. I was there eight weeks, and what one can learn in eight weeks about a place practically the size of a continent is very little. I have been back ten or eleven weeks and, as you know, a lot has happened in that time, but I had a wonderful chance, perhaps a chance very few people have had, at any rate in this land because certain things happened during my visit there. I was given a special pass with a photograph on one side and a notice on the other side to say that I was on no account to be arrested and my photograph was put up in 800 police stations in Moscow and that meant I could go where I liked and there was a great change after that because after that if I spoke to a Russian who knew a little English I did not find a policeman coming after me. Before that I was not allowed to go out of the Embassy or to the shops or to go about and it was very difficult, but after I got the pass I learned more, first on the official side and secondly on the unofficial side. Before I went out I tried to read everything and it seemed to me that everyone was very much prejudiced in one way or the other. They wore certain glasses, either dark spectacles and they saw nothing good, or rosy spectacles and whatever brutalities went on saw only the best and it seemed to me that there must be a middle line. My children laughed and said, "Dad you went out a most confirmed Tory that ever was and you have come back fifty per cent Bolshie." I have come back with a most wonderful admiration and no one has stressed the marvellous things they have done, the marvellous planning and discipline, brutal and ruthless but quite marvellous.

I am going to tell you what will interest you most that I saw in the eight weeks that I was there. I am not going to take more than forty minutes and in that time I will try and tell you about the things that will interest you most.

I will tell you a little bit about their fire-watching and a little bit about their town planning, building, education, propaganda, all very wonderful, and as far as one can guess – one was not allowed to see very much – their military preparations. I was very lucky and found a man who had been doing similar work to what I had been doing in the Artillery and he opened his mind very freely to me and told me a lot of things that even the General was not told and he gave me a good deal of information about the artillery side.

I have with me eight copies only of what is called The Midnight Watch.[1] On the right hand side there are pictures of fire-watching in a small block of flats in Moscow. I will divide these up and please pass them round as they might be useful when I am talking about this particular subject.

To take up fire-watching first: I, of course, have had to do with the whole of the fire-watching plans of this country from the very start, and to come back, as I did, some eleven weeks ago and to find the confusion and mess going on was perfectly pathetic after what one has seen in Russia because here there is no discipline and no central body to give an order that something should be done but they tell the local authorities this ought to be done, and the local authorities more or less tell people what they ought to do and there is no central authority which says that so and so shall be done and to shoot them if they do not do it. That is the trouble. You will say I am ruthless. I am not, but let me tell you something about fire-watching in Moscow.

Everyone is conscripted for fire-watching from 15 to 50, men and women, because there is no difference and men and women do the same except wielding the sledge hammer but they do ordinary brick-layers work, carpentry, street cleaning and everything. There are regulations. If you are not on duty or if you disobey orders you are subject to six months imprisonment or fined up to a thousand roubles, but if you are absent from your post after the siren has sounded you are treated as a deserter in the face of the enemy and so shot. They see no hardship in that whatsoever.

I will give you a very typical case. One day I went into a shop and when I went to buy anything I used to pretend I was more stupid than I am and could not buy a handkerchief without having someone who could speak English and then I used to ask about this that and the other thing, and on this occasion there was a girl whom I asked about fire-watching and she said "I do it once in fourteen days here and once a week at home". I said, "That is very hard as it is two nights one week and one night the next" and she said, "Yes". I asked her if she had to be there and she said, "Yes, and if I risked it and they had no warning it would be all right but if there is a warning and I am not there I am shot", and she said, "I have two brothers and cousins serving at the front and if they are not on duty they are shot and I do not want to be treated better than they are. That is reasonable in war-time."

I will give you another case. In the first raid on Moscow we had no bad fire and in the second we had 19, and in the third we had a very bad fire and it burnt out a huge linoleum factory. A military tribunal carried out an enquiry and decided that as the fire had occurred the fire-watching was not as good as it should have been and so they shot the chairman of the company, the managing director and the works manager and a man who was called the house-man was sent to prison. They put that in the orders the next day that the following had been shot for failing to carry out fire-watching at a certain factory. We all thought how horrible it was but I got to know the man in charge of the fire defence of Moscow and I asked him what was the watching in that place like. He said, "We do not know. We do know it was burnt out but some said the fire-watching was all right and some that it was not and so they shot three men and gave another ten years imprisonment." I said, "What about the wives and families of the men?" and he said, "What are the feelings of the wives and families of three men compared with the safety of Moscow. We did it deliberately as we wanted to make an example and the watching is all right now."

That is the line he took, and he did not care about the three men and the feelings of three wives and families if they could make their city safe, and of course they did make their city safe, and never on any of the nights' raids had they more than four or five big fires and I have seen thirty or forty handled by those watchers and they have to have a person on the roof and they have to have people inside as well as people on the roof of the smallest building, and even if it is a single house with four rooms someone has to be on the roof at night. There was a big place like Selfridges where I could see fourteen people on the roof, twenty-four inside in the nether loft and another twenty-four in the basement as a support so that place was employing about sixty-two people every night and they caught their fires. I do not know whether you have ever seen an incendiary bomb fire start as I have seen it in a London fire. It starts as a white glow and then the red glow follows. I saw Bridgewater House and it started with a white glow and then there was a red glow and twenty minutes later the whole place was alight. I never saw that in Moscow and I never saw a big fire start but I saw forty or fifty times the white glow and nothing more. There was an immediate attack and the bomb was thrown out of the window or dealt with by sand but I never saw the white glow followed by the red. And that is the answer. Where there is sufficient strength one can stop the fires, and they see that they have tremendous man power. They do it by employing women and why we do not, I do not know, but that is the policy. It is not easy where one has small rows of houses with many evacuated and where the man power is very low, but where you have large flats one might have a group of 480 people available for watching and one could have ten or twelve for one night so that it would only come round once a month and that helps out.

Their fire brigade is very efficient and very strong – five thousand peace time men for Moscow and the peace time men for London were about eighteen hundred so that a place of about one-fifth of the size had close on three times as many men. They have not increased their strength and there is no A.F.S. [Auxiliary Fire Service] but they have doubled the hours of duty of the fire brigade and instead of getting one day off in four they get one day off in eight which doubles their available strength, but for the fire defence of Moscow they have no A.F.S. Their fire-watchers can deal quickly with fires and they can put out seventy-five to eighty per cent of them.

The brigade is curiously run. It is a very strong party affair, which means that something like sixty per cent are party members. It is run by a sort of regulation. There is very little punishment and fining but if a man did not do the job it could be made unpleasant.

I saw a case where a small fire was handled very brilliantly and I had never seen any order but shortly afterwards I was taken to a fire station where there was a red star on the wall and that station had got a commendation for handling the fire in the way it had done and no other station except the headquarters station had three red stars and they were all out to get three.

Let me tell you how easy it was for them to do it, more easy for them than for us, because they have a central body whereas we say to local authorities, this will be the thing to do and please get on with it, and local authorities get on with it all right, some have and some have not, but in Moscow every house has a house manager and he will be a paid full time man in a group of houses, even wooden houses, some of which still exist in Moscow. Probably ten or fifteen houses will appoint a head who will be house manager for the group. He has a lot of jobs. He is the police spy who reports to the police anything going on wrong or anything improper, or if there is any doubtful person. That is one job and he is entirely responsible for everything in the flats or the houses. If the electric light goes wrong or the water, one does not send for an electrician or a plumber but one tells him and he puts it right and the State pays for it and if he does not you can report him and he will find he has lost his job or find himself in gaol. Therefore you have the house manager responsible for everything in the flats, and he can report anyone for not keeping a flat clean. He is responsible for cleaning the passages and stairs, and looking after the water, electric lights and drains, and if anything is found wrong in his flats he is either turned out of his job or may find himself in prison. At the same time he has the power to order the occupants of flats to do certain things and if they think they are harshly treated they can appeal to the district house manager.

Let me tell you how they do things. Take the job of first-aid. In our billet – we were in the old Czechoslovakian Legation, nineteen of us and we had vast numbers of servants who looked after us. There was a butler and two sort of footmen and chamber maids, and perhaps thirty or forty people looking after us nineteen. Well the house manager took nine of them and said, "You will go and have an ambulance course." Let me tell you what that was. It was twenty-four nights in their own time, with two hours each night, that is forty-eight hours training. There was no tomfoolery, and nothing like what we think is good enough and the people were highly trained people. He said to them, all right, one of you shall keep a watch every night and you must sleep in your clothes in a bed in the refuge and you will keep sterilised water by you all the time and they had to keep the sterilised water going. We had a bad accident and a man fell downstairs and hurt his leg badly. I never saw anything so quick as the way in which that was dressed. The girl on duty, as soon as she saw the cut called the ambulance and cleaned the wound and started to dress it and we heard the ambulance bell at the door. One of the assistant house managers, quite a good man, said we will pick him up and take him to the ambulance. She said, "You will do nothing of the sort. It is my case and you do not interfere in any way" and they waited until the ambulance men came in and they took the man away. That is very typical of the rest and that girl had a job to do and would not let anyone interfere with her because she said she would be responsible. That is how they work and they almost diagnosed diseases every night.

Well that is on fire-watching and first-aid, and now I want to tell you a little about plans for Moscow. I was very lucky in being able to get a book by Sir Ernest Simon who was out in Moscow six years ago and when he came back he wrote a book on Moscow in the making and when he heard that I was going out to Moscow, he managed to get the book to me at the aerodrome at Hendon before I left and I was very thankful to have it because he and his wife when they had visited Moscow had concentrated on the things at which they were expert. Sir Ernest Simon has been several times Lord Mayor of Manchester and is an authority on town planning and building and now he has come to London to continue that work under Lord Reith with a view to after-war planning. When he was in Moscow he was able to get all their plans and ideas, because they were only ideas six years ago, as to what they were going to do and to my amazement I found that half, perhaps a little less than half, had been done and they told me that if they had not had to spend so much money on preparations for war I would have seen the place a hundred per cent completed. If ever a country wanted peace then it was Russia. They wanted nothing more, for the moment at any rate, than to be left in peace to carry out their schemes, the whole of their planning for Moscow. We do not know whether they meant to go for somebody later. That I do not know but I am quite certain that they did not want war now or when they got it.

Let me tell you a little bit about their plans. You have heard of the Metro. I will not tell you much about it except that it as much an advance on the underground railway as our underground railway is an advance on the Paris Metro and they handle their peak traffic just as easily as the traffic in the afternoon. It is a marvellous show. There is no pushing and no gale of wind behind you. You all come down a wide central corridor or lobby and there are gates at intervals and those gates are immediately opposite where the train pulls up and no one is allowed to enter the platform but when the train comes in a girl in a control tower presses a button and the people can come out and then she presses another button and the other people are allowed to go into the train and the train is only allowed twenty-five seconds in the platform and when it goes another comes in every minute and you can check your watch by it. You could check it with a stop watch and every minute a train comes in. There is not the slightest congestion in the rush hour.

You may have heard of Moscow trams and the idea that if you can get an eyelid there you can get on and hang on the back, but now they have a clever bit of propaganda in that way because four years ago they said to the public, you have suffered from these Moscow trams all these years and said nothing but now we are going to take the profits of the last twenty years and ear-mark the profits for the next twenty years and get you something better. And they sent people round the world and they found that Buenos Aires had the best trolley buses and they said that they would have them for Moscow and Moscow did not forget to tell you and said, "We have suffered very much but now you have not anything as good as this". They are very like green line buses and very comfortable and there is room for two people on each side and each person has an armed chair seat. It is another two feet wider and very comfortable running on giant tyres which slows them up a little bit but makes the going very good and they point that out to you.

Another thing is the Moscow–Volga canal. I do not suppose everyone has heard of it. It is within three miles of the length of the Panama Canal and nine times longer than the Manchester Ship Canal and we know nothing about it. Why was it done? largely to bring good water to Moscow. The Volga water is beautifully soft and they say that it is one of the best drinking waters in Russia but they thought that if they were bringing it to Moscow they might as well make it deep enough to carry big boats and they found the Moscow river was not good enough and so they raised the banks by five feet and the bridges and then they said we will concrete the banks in and they then made broad walks along it and so from the fact of making the Moscow canal the river was deepened and the river bridges heightened and the banks concreted in.

Let me tell you how clever the propaganda is. We were coming home from Archangel and I went to a tea shop and the girl serving spoke a little English and she said, "Have you seen our Metro?" And I said, "Have you a Metro in Archangel?" and she said, "I mean the Metro in Moscow" and that girl five hundred miles from Moscow knew about the Metro there and spoke about it – as "my metro" and if you can persuade her that the Metro belongs to her you have gone a long way. I wonder if an Aberdeen girl would talk about "our underground railway in London"? But she made it clear that it was hers. "It is the State's but I am the State." They got the money out of the trams to pay for the buses and it did not go to the hands of any international financiers. They are very right about that because before the revolution the Moscow trams belonged to Americans and it was American capital and they lost the whole lot. But they are watching that does not happen again. They say, "It is our trams, our underground, our Volga Canal – it belongs to me because it belongs to the State."

Now a little bit about education because I have a line on that. Lady Simon did the educational side and I have made every enquiry about that that I could and I was helped tremendously by the Commissar of Education and he gave me information on everything I wanted to know and said that anything in his department that I wanted to know I should ask about and it should be told. You have to be careful because certain people are told to tell you what they want you to know and the person is nothing but a propaganda merchant and the only thing to do in that case is to try to check up what they tell you through some other means, and I will give you two cases to show you how it was done.

The head chambermaid in our billet was a girl of nineteen. She had many older people under her but she was the head one and she spoke English fluently. I will tell you her life history. When she passed out of the village school her papers were sent to Moscow. Everybody has passing out papers which are seen in Moscow. It does not matter whether he is in the heart of Siberia but every child that passes out has his papers examined in Moscow. She was a farmer's daughter four hundred miles from Moscow and keen on English. The mistress of the village school wanted to learn English and so they worked together. When her papers were seen it was said, "This girl knows English" and she was sent to Moscow and she was sent through a higher grade school doing nothing but English and at the end of that time they said "Do a year for us" and during that year she got no money but she was sent to the English Metropole Hotel to help with visitors and a year later when the girl was nineteen when we all came out to Moscow, because she could speak English she was chosen and she said, "I shall never be anything under a head chambermaid. I shall be found a job as head chambermaid for once they have given you a job if you can carry a job you will never be put down to a lower grade and do you recognise what that means to me? I should have been left out on that farm and never come to Moscow at all if the State had not looked after me."

Then there was another case of a girl. I think her father was a clerk and that girl did a typically Russian thing. She decided to learn English so that she could read Dickens in the original and she did that up to eighteen and when she passed out at eighteen she did a brilliant English paper and lucky for her one of things was to write a thesis on the life of an English author and she chose Dickens and it was a big success. She was given five years at the university on modern languages and she is now head of the English section of the bureau on cultural relations with foreign powers with seventeen interpreters under her, and she also interpreted for us and it was very technical and difficult. She had a wonderful voice and an attractive flat for which she pays the same as she would for a slum flat and there you are given a flat according to your value to the State and she is given seats for the opera whenever she asks for them. Most people get seats once a month and also she has a free pass on the railways when she wants to go away. She has six weeks in the Crimea or the Caucasus every year because she is a highly valued member of the State. The people in her flats are very interesting and there are two generals and the head of the State library, and two shock brigade fitters, men sent round the works to get output and they are given a flat rather like a Park Lane flat with sunk bath at the same rent as a slum flat. Another woman organises the distribution of papers through Moscow. She made a success of that.

Then there is another thing which is interesting and that is elimination. When I was in Russia in 1911 they were not efficient. At that time I was mounting six inch and nine inch guns in Kronstad Harbour and there was nothing more dreadful than to get anything done and the army and the navy and everything else was simply hopeless. They did eventually get those guns mounted but they had no fitter and I do not believe they were fired because I could never get anyone to learn to operate them. But the Russians are efficient now and they must be or they would not have held the Germans up, and that is done by a process of elimination. They try a man out in a job and if he cannot do it they put him down to a level where he can do a job. They had a case like that. They had great trouble to get a man to be chief of the

Moscow fire brigade. The last man was a station officer in Leningrad so that would mean that if the chief of the London fire brigade fell he would find himself a station officer in Birmingham and if he cannot do his job as a station officer he will find himself a fireman. They will not have people holding jobs unless they can do them.

There is the case of the man who designed the Moscow underground railway. He has a most marvellous statue in one of the main railway stations but he cannot run the railway. They tried him for six months and he showed that he had not the brains for running the railway. He is one of the professors of engineering in the university and they have a man who can run the railway.

If you are not capable of your job you will be found a job you can do. They are not going to have a lot of dead wood at the top. They are not going to have a figurehead and someone else running the show. If you cannot do a job they will find you one at a level where you can do it and that is done in the munition factories and the changes in the big munition factories in the four or five years past have been tremendous and there have been changes every four or five months until they get the right man and from what we saw it seems as if they have. I saw some of their munition factories change an A. tube of guns. They can change an A. tube in the factory or in position and they do it in two days. Every battery has two artificers to do that and we know all that now and I know how they do it and I was allowed to see it done and I saw them start on the Monday morning and by lunch time on Tuesday it was done, and I spent most of a day to have a look to see how it was done. That is the line, to get the right people at the head of things and to find a man something he can do and I was told that was pretty general throughout the whole of their services.

The children, as you know, go to school from eight to twelve and when they have done four years it is thought that their teachers should be able to say what sort of line is a good thing for them to follow. The parents have a certain say but the State has the final say. At twelve every child is ear-marked for a certain line and I will tell you what those four lines are briefly.

The first thing which is striven for is to go to a higher grade school until 18 and then do five years at the university – all, of course, paid for by the State. For certain things you must go to the university. You cannot become a doctor or a lawyer without doing those five years at a university and there are certain other things, like the engineering profession which can be helped very much if you can get chosen for a university course. It is the same for a musician: if you want to become a conductor of a State opera it is almost essential to do five years at the university but every child is not equal to that. They have five years at what they call the condona. That is a modified form of university. An architect has to go through that and an engineer has to go to it if he wants to get into any high line of engineering. Accountants have to do that because you cannot be a chartered accountant without that course and certain things of that sort.

Then there is a third thing which is a mixed school and that I saw a lot of and was what one might call a work school. I saw exactly what they do and every big works has to run its own school and a child goes there and has to do three years in the work school because they have general education and they also specialise in any work in which the children are employed. In other words they are training their foremen and draftsmen. You never become a foreman in a big works unless you have gone through a works school or the condona and so through the three years course there is general education, a specialising for Siemen Schucker, or what was that before the revolution, that is the big electrical works in Moscow, and there have studied high grade electricity generating and that sort of thing, and at the age of 19 they go into the works as a draftsman or assistant foreman and they never really go in as workmen.

The fourth stage is when the child is worth nothing better than industry but even there they go to industry at 16 but only half time and no one is allowed to go full time until 18 years of age, and through those two years they are supposed to do, and made to do, a certain amount of work so that at 18 they can pass a certain examination and if they cannot they go into industry but they still have to work to pass it and some of them go on until they are 24 or 25 and they have to work in their own time to get up to a certain standard of education and therefore they are a very educated race of people and it is very interesting to see the types of person one meets that can talk about really deep subjects and books and music, and if you talk to people about books quite a lot knew about English literature and books they would like to read if there were any translations of them. And you can talk about engineering to some of the boys going into engineering and it is amazing the technical knowledge those people have and very different to talking to some of our apprentices. They would know about tools and making things and they would talk about ballistics. They all know something about their job and that is a very good thing.

Perhaps I am painting too glowing a picture and I daresay I am but I can tell you about the brutality of shooting people. I saw a most dreadful thing. I saw a woman killed and it was a perfectly horrible sight. She was arrested in the flats opposite our billet and she came out walking between two policemen without any attempt to escape and they put her in the back of a police van. They were not ordinary police:

the secret police are not nearly so nice. One went forward to speak to the driver and this woman got out of the van and started to go back to the flat. It did not appear to me that she was trying to escape but had forgotten something and was trying to get it and they just killed her. The manager of the billets said that she was endeavouring to escape arrest and if they had gone back without her to the police station they would have been shot for allowing her to escape and they would not take any risk.

There is a lot of prison labour and we saw prison labour gangs finishing a job at night and at six o'clock lorries came for them and took them back to prison and as soon as the whistle sounded the men turned round fast for the lorries and that was not good enough for the guards and they clubbed them and when they got them on the top of an earth rampart they kicked them in the back and it seemed to me utterly unnecessary. They had done nothing to deserve that. It was all utterly bestial and ruthless because women are treated just the same as men.

I do not know whether you have heard of Gorki [sic Maxim Gorky] and the three doctors, but it is common knowledge in Russia and ought not to go outside these four walls. Gorki was Stalin's bosom friend. They say that all Stalin knows Gorki taught him and they were tremendous friends and he died and he had three surgeons attending him, one a very famous Russian surgeon. They had a post mortem and the disease he died of was cancer of the stomach and Stalin stayed in two rooms in the Kremlin for a week and when the week was over he decided to hold a medical enquiry and he held it and he was the only member and those three doctors just disappeared and were never seen again and he shot the three of them. There is no question about it, and that is the sort of person who kicks a dog to get his own back. I have heard a great deal to show that those three men were not in any way responsible for Gorki's death and that is the sort of thing that happens.

Stalin's favourite wife disappeared. She made an unfortunate speech about the Kulaks and said they were being treated much too harshly. She never appeared in public again. They say she committed suicide because he was so horrible to her. We do not know how she committed suicide but she just disappeared and that sort of thing goes on all the time and I cannot help thinking there must be a lack of initiative. I do not see it yet because the war has proved that some of them must have initiative but I cannot help thinking when everybody is ground down like that there must be a lack of initiative.

People ask me whether I saw any sign of leniency towards the church. Some years ago they took down the crosses from the churches and put up the red star instead but now they have allowed them to put back the crosses except in the churches in the Kremlin. They had notices in the papers last Easter that there was no intention of forcing people to go to church and if anyone wanted to go to church it would not be considered against them and as a consequence the Russian churches were packed full. There are two sects, the Greek Orthodox and the Greek non-Orthodox, and they have been told that they are not to squabble about religion or the whole thing would be reconsidered but if they do not squabble people can go to church so there is an easing off there. It is undoubtedly the case as I saw the only churches left with the red star are the two churches in the Kremlin and they cannot bring themselves to alter that, but all the churches outside have got crosses so there we see a great sign of easing.

Another thing is house property. If you save money you can buy a bit of land to buy a house. You could not do that eighteen months ago but now you can but the moment you finish it the Government make a valuation although you can employ a valuer to check up and the State pays the value of the house as soon as you leave it and so if the value of the land goes up the State makes a profit and if it goes down the State loses. You can leave the house to your wife or children, or their children can leave it to their children and go on enjoying the use of the house as long as you like but you cannot sell it for it belongs to the State if you want to sell it and if you want to leave they will hand you the value and that is really allowing a propertied class but not allowing them to make a profit out of their investment.

One sees signs of that in another thing. It was said to me by someone who had studied history quite a lot and was one of the greatest experts in party history in Russia, and he talked to me quite a lot about the shootings and so on because, of course, when they shot generals they shot sixty per cent of all above colonel's rank and those so shot were undoubtedly German tainted and had German leanings. He told me that it was the cutting out of dead wood to save the tree. I suggested that it sounds awful and he said "Well we are a very young nation. The revolution is only twenty years old and nothing happened for eight or nine years except complete chaos and we are really only ten or eleven years old, and" he said, "when you were a child of ten or eleven were you allowed many ideas of your own?" I said "No, but the children of ten or eleven in England now are allowed ideas of their own." He said, "Cannot you see it is much the same thing with us who are a young nation and we have to teach them that it is their duty to obey and we teach them party history which is all that we want them to know." I said, "Does that mean that when they are grown up they will have a greater say?" He said, "Perhaps they will but I am not going to say" and he mentioned about the church.

Two more things and I am stopping. One is the Finnish war. I wonder whether you realise that was a complete bluff for they never meant to finish that war quickly. They put in their poor regiments and field guns and did not put up any good tanks, and after a time Timoshenko went up and finished it exactly fourteen days from the time he went up and I believe that was pure bluff. They did not mind losing three or four thousand men to bluff Germany into thinking that they were thoroughly inefficient and I put that to the Governor of Moscow and he said he would not deny it and that if the army could not beat Finland could they hold the Germans as they are now doing?

I got another line on that. The German military attache wanted to see a tank factory and they refused to let him see one but eventually the ambassador said that they must and the Russians said, "We will give you one hour unescorted in our tank factory" and they fitted up a dud tank factory for him to see and they took a firm making electric radiators and got it to turn out a few tanks and there they let him be for an hour and he begged for two hours and they let him have an hour and a half. At another place nearby there was a big tank factory where they were turning out forty a month and people who go to that length will go a very long way.

The unfortunate thing is that they were so stupid with us and would not tell us what they were doing and would not tell the generals who went out there and maintained their secrecy, and it seems to me that for the last five or six years it has been their intention to fight Germany. They have not been doing this to fight Turkey or China or Japan and everything has been for the coming German war. You can see that and if only we had known that and they had told us what they were up to I cannot help thinking it would have been easier for us to have got together before the last moment, but they would not tell us and they would not tell me about the A.R.P. [Air Raid Precautions] or the fire fighting for three weeks.

I have a few photographs, including some of the Kremlin. Some people think the Kremlin is an ancient building. It is 25 acres in extent. It is like a city with every sort of thing. The photograph on the top here is the Kremlin and down below in the right hand corner is the Kremlin with camouflage and it is one of the cleverest things I have ever seen in my life. The whole of that is camouflage and when I tell you that those streets are only a canvas painted by stage carpenters, all on a single sheet of canvas, you will see the marvellous perspective those people can do. The others are not so interesting as they are fires. I do not think I have anything else to talk about.

One thing you ought to know. When the City of London was burnt Sir Christopher Wren's plan for rebuilding the City was three semicircular roads and three broad roads running out from it and Moscow's plans are exactly the same only there are seven circular roads and seventeen streets running out of it. They are over 100 metres wide and they have completed five out of the seven circular roads and eleven out of the seventeen radial roads.

It is not as difficult as it sounds. The centre is already built up. There are no 99 year leases and all the land belongs to the State and if they want to pull houses down they can do so. After the centre, for the next four miles, there are wooden houses and then for the next eleven or fifteen miles out there are modern flats and workmen's dwellings.

Plans have been made for the building of the roads which are 100 metres wide so that the building of them sounds a difficult matter but it is interesting that Wren's plan for the City of London is almost identical with their plan for Moscow but their plan was on a much vaster scale. Wren only considered the City of London and they are considering Moscow which is one-fifth of the size of the City of London, and, as I say, they have already built five out of seven circular roads and eleven out of seventeen of the radial roads.

I have talked a full forty minutes and I hope I have not bored you.

Discussion

CHAIRMAN: The meeting is now open for question and discussion.

QUESTIONER: Did you see anything on the humanistic or cultural side of education? Did you ever see an elementary school and have explained what the content was and what they are taught about foreign history?

COLONEL SYMONDS: I tried to do that but I cannot read Russian but the flats all have a children's corner, even if the parents live in one room, and they have a corner set aside for children's homework and while that goes on the parents go out and leave them. I did go with an interpreter and saw a boy of about twelve and a girl about eleven and the boy was doing arithmetic and for a boy of twelve doing quite advanced arithmetic, and the little girl was doing natural history and that was frightfully well illustrated and the book she had was marvellously illustrated but when you cannot read a word of Russian it is very difficult.

As regards foreign countries, I do not know what children are taught but I know what adults are taught and are thinking and they have not much use for any of us. They are willing to be allied with us but do not approve of our methods. Where it hurts is that certain papers have criticised their way of life and their politics and the Governor of

Moscow said, "You can go through the last five years of Pravda (the big newspaper) and I will give you fifty roubles every time you see a criticism of English life or English politics or anything of that sort." I said, "All right let us do it" and I should be sorry to do the same with The Times or the Daily Telegraph as I would not have much money to take back to England. I said, "There is nothing in it". He said, "There is a lot in it. Why should England tell us what to do and what not to do and if they let us carry on with our own way we should be better pleased."

We are not popular but the first language now is English and the second German, the third Italian and the fourth French, and that has all come in the last four months. A person has practically got to learn English and then to take German, Italian and French if they wish to, and the change is from German because it was German, English, Italian, French, and now it is English, German, Italian, French, and they have to have English. It is a language they have practically got to learn but I was not able to find out what they were teaching their children about foreign affairs.

QUESTIONER: How large is the wooden area between the centre of the city and the suburbs?

COLONEL SYMONDS: The centre of the city is all stone and concrete and is 2 ½ miles. Then there is 4 ½ to 5 miles of wooden buildings and then you start the flats which go out to about 15 miles but it is the intention and plan that the outer city should grow and the wooden buildings will all go.

QUESTIONER: Are not the wooden buildings a danger for fires?

COLONEL SYMONDS: Not as great as they seem. They are log buildings and not frame buildings and they insist on a forty foot fire break between buildings. They say that a wooden house often goes up but a fire does not spread to the other log buildings, but with an American town of frame buildings it is another story. They say that if it had not been for the preparations for the war there would have been few wooden buildings now and you can see where they have been pulled down and central flats have grown up.

QUESTIONER: That is marvellous because in the last war they were mainly wooden buildings.

COLONEL SYMONDS: They are not allowed now in the centre to have wooden buildings.

QUESTIONER: Have they considered the difficulties of Washington? The people have the circular plan there and are not satisfied. I am told that Washington people do not like that form of building.

COLONEL SYMONDS: From what I saw it is a marvellous arrangement for quick moving traffic and if you can move traffic swiftly round the different circular roads it is surely going to stop congestion in the centre of Moscow and I thought it was a very fine plan, as far as one could see it looked a very fine plan but I do not know whether Washington may have something better.

QUESTIONER: I like Washington very much but I was surprised to hear they are not satisfied.

COLONEL SYMONDS: How wide are their streets?

QUESTIONER: Very wide.

QUESTIONER: It is interesting that you state the people are housed according to their capabilities and that their generals are housed in Mayfair flats but are they housed according to their value to the State as they get on in life and their value goes down?

COLONEL SYMONDS: The age at which you have to take a pension is very carefully laid down. The most I know is that the girl who is on cultural relations has to give up at 52 and she told me that of course normally she would be expected then to have a small house well outside Moscow and a pension sufficient for her to live and if she was sufficiently lucky she would have a retaining fee to advise her department and they do quite a lot of that, and if a man retires – and I think a man retires at 55 – if he has done very well he is given a retaining fee to advise his department but they do not let people hang on and at a certain age you have to go and they pension you and give you a house and she said it would be a nice little house. Her only complaint was that she would not be able to go into Moscow as much as she would like, or as much as she like's to do now as she loves opera. She spends every minute of her life in the State library and if I rang her up at the State library I could always find her.

QUESTIONOR: Do they have no choice in the houses they have?

COLONEL SYMONDS: Yes, it depends a good deal on their work and if they are working in a certain area in Moscow they would try to put them near their work but if that cannot be done they are given a pass on the trams or railway or underground from their work to place of residence and they give the wives a pass three times a week for shopping and it is rather interesting, if you buy a cinema ticket in Moscow it is a pass on the tram. Of course the opera ticket is too and if you go into the central cinema in Moscow and buy a ticket, if you live ten or fifteen miles out it is a pass on the trams. I do not think they have a lot of choice and they are probably told where they have to go. I am told one of the officers on the General Staff thought it very hard that he had to go ten miles out and although he had a car it was a great hardship and I said, "Cannot you appeal?" and he said, "Oh no, you will only get into trouble if you do that" and he said, "I will get in later again and it is one of the things you have to put up with." He was a major on the General Staff, a person who could pull strings if anyone could and he said that it did not pay and if you grumble there is a black mark against you and that he would do what he was told.

They were widening a street before the war started and all the people living in the heart of Moscow over their shops had been cleared out twelve or fourteen miles out, and I do not think there is any option. You are not asked to criticise but to do just what you are told.

QUESTIONER: Then they really live in fear?

COLONEL SYMONDS: Yes, no doubt they do live in fear.

QUESTIONER: What happens to children up to the age of eight?

COLONEL SYMONDS: There is no State school but if they are invalids they are taken away quite young from their parents. I do not fancy, except for school at home, they get any regular schooling up to eight. There are no kindergartens as far as I could see at all.

That matter of fear is rather interesting because they do not look happy. You never see a happy looking Russian. I tried to find out whether they were always like that and a representative of the Daily Telegraph who had been there for forty years, or someone who had been there over thirty years, said that they never looked happy like our Cockneys but they do live in fear.

QUESTIONER: Their lack of happiness was always portrayed in their literature.

COLONEL SYMONDS: No, there is not much happiness in their literature. I do not think they are a happy people but they are a very healthy people. We took the film "London Can Take It" and there were a lot of white faces and sick looking people coming up from the dug-outs and the white faces of children in dug-outs and I said that to show that in a town like Moscow cannot be done, and that picture was done deliberately to show what we looked like after a year of bombing but even so I do not think we did look like that after a year of bombing and I was told that the harm had been done but I said it should not have been shown.

They decided about three years ago that Moscow did not get enough vegetables or fish so they laid out about five million (?) acres round Moscow entirely for vegetables and the consequence is you can buy a very nice cucumber, not a long one but rather a round one, for a penny, and a cauliflower for a penny. And five fish trains a day come from the North and the fish shops have something like a barber's pole which they can put up when fresh fish is in and then people go and get the fresh fish. It is usually sturgeon and between fourpence and fivepence a pound, all very fresh and there is no middleman and the State bring it down from Archangel, I think, and the people can buy it.

The people are very healthy and look awfully well. And I like their dresses too. Some girls try to wear European or English dress but their own dress is very attractive, very simple and with bright colours.

QUESTIONER: Do you think other towns have been treated in the same way as Moscow?

COLONEL SYMONDS: We were told that. I wanted to go to Leningrad to see what A.R.P. they had there but they said that when Moscow decides to do a thing Leningrad and everybody else will do the same thing.

QUESTIONER: May I ask one final question about your very interesting talk? I would like to know whether the reports that come out in the paper saying over and over again when Moscow is raided by aeroplanes that only one or two get through, is that really a fact?

COLONEL SYMONDS: Yes, I think it is. I have to be careful because if I say too much I will tread on the toes of my own people. It is true that the barrage they put up did prevent the Germans getting through. You have to remember three things. They have to fly three hundred miles over unfriendly country, and it is very unfriendly country because I would be very sorry to any German compelled to bale out or who was a parachutist because they have issued the people with shot guns as far as they can go. Secondly, the Germans are so frightened of the Russian fighters that they will only go in the dark and as it was not dark till 9.30 and light again at 2.30 it did not give them very long to go the 300 miles, drop their bombs and get back. You can work that out for yourselves. No doubt the bulk of the bombs dropped were outside the barrage line and the outer barrage is twelve miles out and the woods beyond that are pitted with bomb craters and far more bombs were outside the Moscow barrage than inside and the Russians said that they thought that 200 planes tried to get in and I know from my place in the centre of Moscow that never more than twelve got in, twelve or thirteen at the very outside. But they had everything against them, bright nights which aided the gunners and a tremendously heavy barrage. I think the barrage round Moscow, compared with London, was three times as great for a place one-fifth of the size so that it was really fifteen times as heavy. They have a centre, an inner circle and an outer circle and the inner circle fire to the same ring and the outer barrage do not do anything of the sort and simply put up a curtain of fire and simply plaster the sky with stuff. I do not know how clever it was because you do not know what they are up to but on the first night the planes came low and the anti-aircraft fire brought down fifteen of them, and I saw ten of them. Then they came high after that and few of the Russian guns could range them and then the Russians brought naval guns with a ceiling of 32,000 feet. They smashed every window in the neighbourhood but the Russians put wood in the windows and said that the people would have to put up with it, and the Germans could not go above 32,000 feet.

We picked up in one night at my billet, which is 22,000 square feet, or three or four times the size of this house, sixteen pounds weight of shells, or forty-two pieces of stuff. I have been out a good deal and spent a lot of time at the Home Office and I have never had anything like that. They were putting up a tremendous barrage. That was eight or eleven weeks ago and I am quite sure in the time I was there in nineteen raids which I saw that not one-tenth of the planes got through that tried to get in but unloaded their bombs outside the barrage altogether. We spent the whole day with the American Ambassador in the woods outside and the whole of the wood was pitted with craters and you never saw anything like it.

The worst raid in Moscow was when there were thirty-two high explosives and sixteen fires in one night, that is fires which the brigade had to attend to. The thirty-two bombs were mostly small stuff, 250 lb bombs. Apparently each plane carries four bombs like that. That is about one thousand kilos load for three hundred miles. That is about what they do and they cannot do more than that for they must have petrol for six hundred miles and that allows them to carry a thousand kilos weight in bombs.

I am hoping that the information they gave us out there as regards bombing is true and I hope their information about the war is true because they do not minimise in any way the damage which was done but they told us when there had been raids and how many buildings had been damaged and as far as one could see it was fairly correct. If they had thirty-two incidents in one night they would allow twenty-eight or twenty-nine of them and they were not minimising and I am hoping they are doing the same with their war communiques.

QUESTIONER: Would it be indiscreet to ask how do you account for the pact between Germany and Russia?

COLONEL SYMONDS: I do not know really what to say but I think they wanted peace at any price and they wanted to be left alone but that did not stop them from making all preparations, pact or no pact, because they knew it was coming. Of course they had enemies and we had a bitter enemy with us, a man who ought never to have been sent out, and he said, "Yes, of course they made that pact to keep out until the end of the war and when both sides were exhausted they were going to attack us through Germany." But that pact was to keep the peace as long as they could because they were not ready and they did not say they were ready. As the Governor of Moscow said, "You are never ready, we were not ready but it is no good saying we were not when attacked. It is all very well to say you are not ready but if you are attacked like they attacked us you have to be ready." The Governor is the right man in the right place and almost the last thing he said was "Symonds, have you thought that this is a wonderful place to defend. All my walls are about three feet six inches thick. By Jove, we are going to defend Moscow all right. They will never get into Moscow." I do not believe they ever will any more than they got into Leningrad. They were issuing shot guns to the ladies for Nazi parachutists and they told them that they would be given five rounds of ammunition and five clay pigeons for practice on a certain day. We started off but because every woman in Moscow turned up with a shot gun we could not get near the place and they said that they could not do it and asked everyone whose Christian name started with A. to come on Monday, and those whose names started with B. on Tuesday, and so on, and when they got started we went out and there they were with spring guns shooting at clay pigeons and not doing too badly. There was a big canvas screen and on the other side rifle fire was going on and those women were going in under the screen and I said, "Have you rifle practice?" I was told "only shot guns" but they are going to have full rounds for rifles because they armed them in Leningrad before we left and the Germans were twenty-two miles from Leningrad and no doubt the women will fight in the line in Moscow, and they will give them a flat cap and a rifle and tell them, "Just go and shoot Germans", – just like that.

One thing I did forget was that we were given a marvellous Russian dancing show. Old Russian dancing is a really wonderful show and in the middle a man who had written a little play came on and they clapped him and he said, "Now thank you very much but there are a lot of English officers here. Don't you think we ought to clap them?" And they did not make much response but on came a commissar in charge of the theatre who said, "Either you did not understand what that man said or you forgot to clap." The State approved their clapping the English officers but the public were not sure whether they ought to clap or not.

THE CHAIRMAN: When you began your delightful and interesting talk you said that you could talk for hours but you would only give us forty minutes to-day. I give you full warning that we will let you off because quite definitely we want you to come and talk to us again and I am quite sure I am interpreting the feelings of everybody here when I say we have been completely thrilled by everything you have told us and we have thoroughly enjoyed all you have said.

Note

1 A poster was published by the British Ministry of Home Security in 1942 called The Midnight Watch, about British fire-guards and civil defence workers. It may have been based on the Russian poster referred to here.

LECTURE NINE

Siberia

By Countess Czarkowska
Lecture on 15 April 1942

Introduction

In August 1939 Nazi Germany and the Soviet Union signed a pact to divide up Poland between them, leading to the start of World War Two the following month. Poland was invaded from the east by the Soviet Union on 17 September, but it was not until the following Spring that large numbers of Poles were transported to Siberia and other parts of the Soviet Union to work as forced labour. There were three waves of deportations and Countess Czarkowska,[1] a married woman, was part of the second wave when about 330,000 Poles were taken forcibly from their homes on the night of 12 April 1940. The Countess was taken from her home in Lwow, with her two small children, aged four and six, and transported to the Kazakhstan area of Siberia.

This lecture describes her life in Siberia on a collective farm (*kolkhoz*) from 1940 to 1941 during the harshest winter for decades. In spite of appalling conditions, the Countess was remarkably free from bitterness about her experiences and she did not condemn Russia, in fact she said that 'personally I have no complaint against the Soviet authorities, with which I never had any trouble'. She spoke Russian, having lived in the Ukraine during the World War One. Her lecture was not labelled 'confidential', and although it was not published in the Journal, it was open for debate and wider discussion. It has been suggested that the Countess may have been trying to protect friends and relatives still in Russian-held territory at the time of her lecture. Another remarkable statement came from the RCAS Chairman, Lord Hailey, who said the Countess's account described 'something of these great operations that Russia has carried out in the way of colonising these Asiatic areas'. Hailey had been Governor of the Punjab during his distinguished Indian career. We can only specu-late on whether he genuinely thought Stalin's policy of forced collectivisation was a novel attempt at colonisation, or that he was, like the Countess, protecting people still in danger. It is also possible that staff from the Soviet Embassy in London had been invited to the lecture. Certainly lecturer, chairman and the single questioner all seemed at pains not to be negative about the Russian ally in public, whatever they thought in private.

By the summer of 1941 the political and military scene had greatly changed. Germany had invaded Russia in June, and a treaty was quickly drawn up in London between the Soviet Union's ambassador and the Polish Government in exile. An amnesty was announced on 12 August for all Poles in the Soviet Union (deportees and prisoners-of-war) and men were encouraged to join the Polish Army set up under General Anders to fight the Nazis alongside the Red Army.

The Countess was freed by the amnesty and according to internal evidence from the lecture, arrived in Britain by ship with her children (probably via the 'Persian Corridor' to Teheran). She was joined by her husband, who seems to have joined the Polish Army in Russia, then the Free Polish Forces in Britain.

ROYAL CENTRAL ASIAN SOCIETY
Report of a Meeting held in The Royal Empire Society's
Assembly Hall, on Wednesday, 15th April, 1942, at 1.30 p.m.
Handwritten note on page 1: Countess Czarkowska[1]
transported to Kazakstan from Lvov by Russians
in September 1939. Not published.
Chairman: Lord Hailey

THE CHAIRMAN: Ladies and Gentlemen, I have to perform what is the very pleasurable task of the Chairman, that is, to introduce to you your lecturer to-day, the Countess Czarkowska. I know that what she is going to tell you is so interesting that I need say very little indeed in the way of preliminary.

It is interesting from a number of points of view. For instance, Madame in 1939 was taken from Poland by Russians and sent to Siberia. This vast transfer of people, hurriedly, without preparation, no arrangements made, that is the kind of thing which must seem to us in our old settled conditions here, uninvaded, a country that has never been disturbed by these great movements, a most appalling thing, a thing difficult for us to realize.

In the second place, it is interesting because Madame, placed hurriedly in the midst of a very primitive population in Siberia, had to live their life, share with them their primitive conditions. She is one of the few educated people who have really lived that life on the communal farm in conditions of that nature.

It is interesting again because she will be able to tell us something of these great operations that Russia has carried out in the way of colonizing these Asiatic areas. It is fortunate that after the German invasion Madame was brought back again by the Russian Government, and she is perhaps one of the very few Polish ladies who have succeeded in making their way to Great Britain. You will be glad to hear that her husband, who was fighting there, has also found his way here and is fighting in the Polish forces.

There, I think, I have offered you in advance a picture of something that ought to be of superlative interest to you. I will not delay you further, but I will ask Madame to give her address. *(Applause.)*

THE COUNTESS CZARKOWSKA: Since June 22nd 1941 the eyes of more or less the whole world are turned on Russia. Anyhow it has been so until Japan broke into the war. Russia is a part of the world comparatively unknown to people of this country. Perhaps some people know a good deal of the pre-revolutionary Russia. Myself I have had the opportunity of seeing a good deal of the Russia of to-day. During the 1914 war I spent four years in the Ukraine, near Kiev, and lately, as you know, I have lived for eighteen months in a "Kolchoz" i.e. a collective farm in Siberia, as a deportee from Poland.

Of course, I cannot attempt to give you a general view of the present life in Russia, and of the economic and social situation of the country, as my experiences are confined to a small rural area. These few words may perhaps help you to understand what modern Russia is like. I think the simplest way to do it will be to give you an accurate account of my life since April 12th 1940, on which day, or rather night, I was taken from my home in Lwow with my two children, aged six and four.

The details of my departure from Lwow, uninteresting in themselves, may interest you as an illustration of the fate of thousands of people, deported in the same way that same night. At 1.30 a.m. five officials of the G.P.U., or the N.K.V.D.,[2] as they are now called, walked into my room and declared, without any particular wrath or cruelty, that I must get myself and the children ready to leave within the next hour and a half for an unknown destination. They advised, or rather ordered, me to take as much clothing and luggage as I could pack during that short time. Personally I wanted to take as few things as possible, being then firmly convinced that I would be robbed of everything, whereas what I left behind might be saved. Eventually just the opposite thing happened. I lived eighteen months in Siberia, chiefly on bartering clothes and especially linen, sheets and bed-dressing, to the people there, whereas everything I left in Lwow was lost.

At 3 a.m. punctually an officer of the N.K.V.D. and five men armed from tip to toe came to fetch us. We climbed into a lorry and drove to the station. There we were crammed into a goods waggon, [sic] where already thirty-three other people were settled, and, in pitch darkness, I had to find a corner to lay down the children and sit myself on one of the suit cases. At dawn, everybody woke up and looked round at his companions in misery. They proved to be all wives and families of Government officials, officers, doctors, in other words civilized and cultured people. Until midday nobody seemed to take the slightest interest in us. About that time, a soldier opened the door, read through a list of names he had brought with him, to see that none of the passengers of the waggon was missing, and asked if we wanted anything. Of course, we asked first of all for water. By the way, each person had brought some sort of provisions, chiefly bread, but nobody had anything to drink. After a while, another soldier came, carrying two buckets, and about an hour later, somebody was called out of the waggon to fetch a pail of water. When this came, we were able to make some tea, which was the only warm thing we had that day. The two buckets were the only domestic arrangements we had for all uses during the whole journey. The next night we moved from Lwow, and thus began a dreary, hopeless journey of thirteen days throughout the whole of European Russia to nearly the heart of Siberia. We managed to settle in the waggon in such a way that everybody had room enough to stretch out for the night, but there was not a yard of free space to straighten one's limbs in any kind of movement. The waggon was always closely shut, and only a tiny window in one corner gave light enough to discern faces and things during the day time. For the night we sometimes were provided with a candle and lantern, but oftener not. Warm food was distributed once in every twenty-four hours, but for some queer reason, seemingly because the cooking was done only at main stations, the time of food-dispensing always happened to be at night, any time between 12 and 5 a.m. I think this was due not to any predetermined desire to be cruel to us, only simply to thoughtless and bad organization. The difficulty of getting water was, I think, the worst of all.

In the early morning of the thirteenth day of our journey, the train stopped longer than usual, and we were told to get out. After waiting for a couple of hours on an empty space some half mile away from the station, we were dumped into a lorry and driven to a small so-called town, which was not our final destination, but where we were supposed to stop for the night. The inn we stopped at was something indescribable, and the ten hours we spent there a real nightmare. There were only two rooms altogether, with eight or ten beds each, already occupied by Kirghiz travellers who happened to stop there for the night. Therefore, the whole of our deportee party, about forty people, had to crouch about in free corners on the floor, wrapped in rugs and coats as best we could. The dirt and the quantity of vermin creeping all over the walls was unbelievable. No food was to be obtained on the spot, so we had to go and get some supper in the public restaurant, "stolowaya," as it is called there. We paid very dear to get some eggs, a substitute for tea (unsweetened) and our own stale bread. After this I laid the children down on the floor close to one another, as best I could, and did the same myself, but I soon realized that it was hopeless to think of going to sleep. About eleven o'clock a crowd of drunken peasants poured into the inn, singing, shouting and knocking about in search of beds and free spaces for a night's rest. Then somebody's suddenly awakened child began to howl, – to cut short, this nightmare scenery lasted about till dawn. The children were asleep by now, but I jumped up at the first rays of the sun, preferring the bitter cold outside to the horrible atmosphere of the inn.

About midday we left Borovoi (that is the name of the place) in a lorry, which took us to our final destination, a village called Michailowka.

By the way, I must mention that the Republic of Kazakstan,[3] situated in South-Western Siberia, is a tremendous stretch of land, almost flat as a table, and whose only landscape consists of limitless, and, with very few exceptions, tree-less steppe. Its present population is mostly composed of deportees from all Russian provinces, former "Kulaks," i.e. well- situated peasants under the Tsarist regime, whose land was expropriated by the Bolsheviks and they themselves deported to Siberia with their families. The old native population of Kazakstan belongs to the Mongolian race of the Kirghizes, now called "Kazachs," which name is not to be mistaken with "Kossacks," the well-known Russian cavalry. These Mongols are to-day strongly out-numbered by the Russian deportee newcomers.

Our arrival in Michailowka was pretty queer. We were dumped out of the lorry in the middle of the village at seven o'clock in the evening and left to look after ourselves. A number of children, dressed more or less in rags, gathered around us and stared with intense curiosity at these strange people, decently dressed (magnificently in their eyes) and clean (in their eyes, although we had not washed properly for a fortnight). As, apart from staring, no other initiative was taken with regard to us, we had to think for ourselves and do something. Well, the obvious thing was to find lodgings. I started house-hunting, and soon came across an old woman with Kirghiz features, sitting in front of her hut, built of mud and manure. She did not understand a word of Russian, but I managed to explain to her that I and my two children wanted shelter for the night. She agreed to take me in, sent her little granddaughter with me to help bring the luggage, and in another half-hour I was looking round my new home, the first of the seven I later stayed in during my Siberian exile.

The hut was a typical Kirghiz one: a low, some four feet high door led to a small, single room, the walls and ceiling of which bore many stains of wet and smoke and enormous spider webs in each corner. Not a single piece of furniture: only a sort of wooden elevation made of planks, on which the people lived, ate, slept and worked at various domestic jobs.

The old Kirghiz woman invited me to tea. I gladly accepted the offer, as we had had nothing warm to eat nor drink since the previous night. I must say that the setting of this tea party was anything but an ordinary one.

Four distinctly oriental, narrow-eyes and yellow-skinned figures, sitting cross-legged on the floor, two men in thick, dirty working-clothes, and two women dressed in bright-coloured velvet or plush tunics, worn on very wide linen skirts, their heads wrapped in curious high turbans, tied under the chin and covering part of the face. The soft singing of the samovar, which is a special Russian kettle for boiling water and making tea, seemed a comforting sound in this dismal, almost completely dark room, in which the only light consisted of a tiny bottle of petrol, and a piece of string in it to act as a wick. Of course, this "lamp" emitted far more smell and smoke than it gave light. And in the midst of all this, my two poor tiny mites, hungry, sleepy and too tired even to be frightened, and myself half stunned by all that had happened and half wondering whether I should or not get murdered and robbed of everything I possessed.

Of course, Michailowka, situated in a purely rural district, had her collective farm. A day or two after our arrival, we (I mean all the exiles from Poland) were summoned to the Kolchoz (collective farm) centre and made to hear and believe that our first and unique duty, now that we had the honour to be Soviet citizens,[4] was to devote all our strength and energy to work for the greater welfare of the Soviet Union. The speech of the Kolchoz president ended by inscribing all the present exiles for work on the collective farm, which work was to start on the next morning. When my turn came to inscribe on the list, I calmly but flatly refused to do so. The reasons I gave were: (1) that I had two little children, who had to be looked after and fed, and which I therefore could not leave on God's mercy for whole days; (2) that my physical strength was absolutely disproportionate to the work performed on the collective farm, and that I would be unable to do it even if I wished to; (3) that I would gladly do any intellectual work, such as teacher of a foreign language (Michailowka had a seven class school) or as clerk in any administration office, (I know Russian fairly well). The President of the Kolchoz and the Secretary of the Sel-Soviet (administrative centre of the village) looked first at one another, then at me, with, I must say, far more embarrassment than anger. They did not at all know how to face and deal with the extraordinary fact of somebody refusing to do what everybody else did, and, choosing the easiest way out of an awkward situation, they did not inscribe me for work on the collective farm, or indeed elsewhere. Later on, I was summoned several times by the Kolchoz bailiff in less civil terms, in fact I was threatened with imprisonment, deportation to the "taigi" (desert steppes and marshes in Northern Siberia), but after a while I learnt to know the local conditions well enough to realize that these threats would never be carried out. I therefore quietly stood my ground, and all that happened was that once, when the President of the Sel-Soviet called me to his office and in a more than usual ill-mannered way wanted to force me to go to work, threatening me with all sorts of dreadful things and thumping his fists on the table, he was sent for by the local N.K.V.D. quarters in Borovoi the following day, was terribly scolded there for uncultured behaviour towards a "foreign citizen" and dismissed from his post of Sel-Soviet president. Of course, this little event had a sound repercussion amongst all the exiles.

But you must not think that because I did not work on the collective farm, I had much leisure to spend my time as best I could. The only care of providing the children's and my own living was often more than I could get through.

The organization of the collective farm itself is very simple. All the land belongs to the farm, that is to the State. Each member of the Kolchoz has only a small plot of land of his own, generally varying from two to five acres, on which to grow potatoes. All the men belonging to the Kolchoz are supposed to work at the farm every day the year round. The women are to work as much as possible, generally they put in three or four days a week, and in winter they stop working altogether, which is not astonishing in Siberian climatic conditions. The only aims and duties of the collective farm are: to grow the staple crops, wheat, rye and potatoes, on a definite strip of land (the Michailowka Kolchoz had 2,000 hectares to cultivate) and breed as much livestock as possible. In autumn of 1940 the farm numbered 1,300 cows, pigs, sheep and horses. In spring 1941 there were only 700 left. The remainder had died of hunger.

The collective farm authorities consist of the President, the Purser, a clerk for general purposes, the farm bailiff and several brigadiers in charge of men and women working-brigades. The collective farm workers do not earn any money wages. At the end of the financial year, generally in December or January, the total of the hours of labour of each worker's family are balanced and each family is supposed to receive its part of the general profits. But this takes place only after the State's contributions, which are extremely high, have been paid, and the Kolchoz authorities have received their share. Of course, all is well when the crops are good, such as in 1938, when a really good dividend was paid, which kept all the village families from starvation during the next two years. But in 1940 and 1941, when I was there, there was practically no dividend at all, because the harvests had been very poor, and after the State and the Kolchoz staff had received their part, there remained nothing to distribute among the peasants. All they received for their whole year's hard work was 400 gr. of bread daily and a few watermelons. Needless to say that occurrences like these do not help to make the collective farm system popular amongst the population, most of which remembers better days, when each man had his own bit of land and the liberty to cultivate it how and when he chose. When the war with Germany broke out, there was one unanimous desire felt, I think, by every one of Michailowka's Kolchoz members: "Whatever the war brings us, let's hope to God it will put an end to the collective farms."

The Sel-Soviet, which I have mentioned several times already, was the political and administrative centre of the village. It numbered four or five Government officials, and its chief aim and duty, besides the purely technical administration of the village, was to watch the political and social atmosphere among the inhabitants. In this respect a curious characteristic of the population is their almost panic fear of the N.K.V.D. (Secret State Police) authorities. This is proved by the fact that in a village of four thousand inhabitants there was only one militia man to keep people and things in order, and this was quite sufficient.

I must say that the chief and most striking characteristic of Michailowka was the general poverty of everybody and everything. For example, but for very few exceptions, the average hut was always built of mud, clay and manure, very small, very low, damp and dark. The average food-stuffs were neither plentiful nor varied. My own diet consisted nearly invariably of coarse, wheat brown bread, of which, I confess, I was personally very fond, dry potatoes, milk, when I could get some, and sometimes butter, lard and eggs. But these were luxuries, which I could very seldom allow myself, and during the second year of my residence they became quite unobtainable for me. But, apart from the fact that my position as an exile, was far worse than that of an ordinary peasant, their standard of living was also terrifically low when compared to this country, if such a comparison is possible altogether. Collective farm workers also only relied on their provisions of grain and potatoes to live on, but then they had at least these two things in more or less sufficient quantity, and added to them their own milk and sometimes butter and cheese, each drop or ounce of which I, for instance, had to buy or barter. Nevertheless, this diet as a basis of nourishment of a whole population cannot be considered as very rich. The lack of vitamins and sugar, which in this country, for example, is the object of constant care and endeavours of amelioration, is absolutely ignored in Siberia and nobody cares about it in any way. No vegetables are to be obtained, except very expensive cucumbers in summer and sometimes a little cabbage and very scarce carrots. Fruit is unknown altogether, except again for very expensive water melons and a kind of berries which grow in the woods but are so sour that nobody can eat them without sugar.

As for fuel, I have already mentioned that the steppe in that part of Siberia is almost treeless, and therefore wood is almost unobtainable. The stock fuel article of the villagers is dried cow dung, first reduced to a state of sticky clay by mixing with water, and then made into a kind of special brickettes, which have to dry in the sun during several weeks. These brickettes are called Kiziak, and I must say that, when properly dried, they burnt quite well and gave sufficient heat to the rooms, though the smell and smoke they spread were terrific, and cooking in stoves thus heated took a discouragingly long time. The other staple fuel article is a kind of grass which grows in great profusion on the steppe. This grass, called poloun, has very thick, hard stalks, and is generally quite dry by September. It is then gathered and stored up as winter fuel in great quantities. I soon got into the habit of going out on the steppe each morning to fetch my provision of droppings or peloun for the day, and sometimes for a few days ahead. The children often came with me and helped me as best they could.

The clothing question in Russia has been spoken of and discussed so often in the whole world, that I think it unnecessary to dwell upon it here. The average peasant's clothes are very poor, very scarce and very expensive. That is the reason why the inhabitants of Michailowka were so anxious to get hold of any garments of the Polish exiles. But they always wanted the thing we bartered to be absolutely new. This is because all the Soviet stuffs are of such bad quality that the people cannot believe that somewhere in the world there can be materials which after a year's use are still worth having.

It is easily comprehensible that in a climate such as the Siberian one the clothing question rises to the level of a very serious and important problem. Weather extremes make life here exceptionally hard. The winter 1940–1 was the worst ever in the recollection of the oldest inhabitants of Michailowka. The snow came on October 1st and lay on the ground till the first of June. The temperature between December 25th and the 5th January fell twice to 70 C. below freezing point. The average temperature during five months maintained itself between 25 and 35 degrees, below freezing point, of course. Siberian snow storms are peculiar to the country. Snow in Siberia never seems to fall in soft mother goose flakes, like it does here. A dry north or north-western wind sweeps down from the Arctic over the bare, tree-less frozen plain, comprising the Siberian steppe, flat as a table, about 1,300 feet above sea level. The powdered snow, driven by the cruel wind, cuts your face and lungs like tiny shreds of powdered glass, and is hell to man and beast not brought up to it.

Summer in Kazakstan is sometimes very hot and dry, as it was in 1940, when we did not get a drop of rain from the 15th June till October 1st. At other times you scarcely have a few warm days during the four summer months altogether, as happened last year. I remember only ten hot days from June to October. I have already mentioned that the chief social characteristic of the village of Michailowka was a deeply rooted, terrific fear of the N.K.V.D. authorities. As in every community ruled by fear, there is a general spying system, so highly developed that practically not a man or woman in Siberia ever believes his or her neighbour, and very often I experienced the fact that peasants, who confidently opened their hearts to me on subjects such as their longing for some other Government or their hatred of the collective farms, first looked very carefully all round, or, if indoors, behind each door and window, to make sure that no uncalled-for ears were near. The curious fact of their speaking frankly to me can, I suppose, be explained by their logical deduction that it would be of no interest whatever to me to denounce their secret feelings to the chiefs, and that besides, having come from a country where I was considerably better off, I probably knew better.

I had a curious experience when I once wanted to sell a gold bracelet, at a moment when, for some reason or other, I wanted a rather large sum of money at a time. Now gold objects, other than coins, are not prohibited by law in Russia, and the wives or sisters of better situated officials and officers often wear gold rings and other jewels. But when I wanted to sell this very pretty and valuable bracelet of mine, I could not for my life find a purchaser. Not that they did not like it or could not pay the, by the way, ridiculous price I asked for it, simply they were terrified by the thought that somebody might denounce them as very rich people who could afford to buy gold jewels. After long and tedious bargaining, I finally did sell it to the head schoolmaster, the only true and active communist I ever met in Russia.

The education in Siberia stands on a very low level, as it does in a very poverty-stricken country. I noticed that nearly all the women above forty were illiterate. The men, on the whole could read and write, but most of them with great difficulty, except, of course, Government officials. School is compulsory for all the children. The subjects taught are reading, writing, arithmetic, geography and history (of the Soviet Union only). In higher classes, Russian literature, physics, algebra, natural history, anatomy and physiology, Godlessness and long paragraphs of what Lenin, Stalin and other contemporary prophets had said or done. About the world, at large, and what exists and happens outside of their own country, nobody seems to know or care. When the treaty of alliance with Great Britain was signed after the German invasion, I accidentally happened to listen to a discussion between the post-mistress, the purser of the Sel-Soviet, a schoolmaster and a fourth person whom I do not remember. They were discussing the following problems: Was England a German, Polish or Russian province?

When they addressed me, I tried to explain as best I could what I thought Great Britain was. The next question was whether Berlin was a British, Polish or German town? To that also I answered satisfactorily. The third enquiry was, whether England was fighting, and, if so, since when and against whom? The people interested, mind you, all belonged to the so-called intelligentsia of the village.

To return once more to my personal experiences, I should like to give you a description of the only time I worked on the Michailowka collective farm. This happened in summer 1941 on a fine morning in July. One of the Kolchoz brigadiers came to the hut where I was living and very politely asked me whether I should come for one day and help do the hay-making. As it was a beautiful day, we were all well and I thought the experience might be an interesting one, I readily answered I should go with pleasure, and taking the children with me I started for the farm at once.

After about an hour's drive in a cart driven by horses we and eight other village women arrived on the part of the steppe where the hay was to be made. The day was really glorious, not too hot, swallows and larks were singing as if they wanted to make up for all the horrors that were going on in the world, and a fresh East wind filled the lungs with healthy, sweet-scented air of the steppe. The children, though bare-footed, were delighted to run about, gather flowers and watch the machine cut the grass or collect the hay ready to be put into stacks. This was the job I was appointed to and worked at, fork in hand, for five or six hours, I must confess not over-tiring myself any more than the true Kolchoz workers did. We had two hours off at dinner-time, and were given a big plateful of soup, a large slice of fresh brown rye bread and a cup of unsweetened beverage pompously called tea. We returned home at seven o'clock p.m., tired, but pleased with the experience, which was not repeated.

Another time I was appointed by the Sel-Soviet to do some road-building, the aim of which was to raise the level of a road which crossed the river in such a way that the water could not overflow it. There were three other women with spades besides myself, and a brigadier to look after us. The work consisted in digging up a spadeful of sand from the side of the road and carrying it some four to five yards further. It was to be thrown in the middle of the road. After doing this for the first half-hour, I asked our watchman, who accidentally [sic, incidentally?] happened to be a very quiet, peacefully minded Kirghiz, if he did not think it would be useful to provide us with a little cart or a couple of wheelbarrows, which could carry a bigger load of sand at a time. The work would thus be speeded up considerably. The man looked at me with frank amazement, and smiling complacently asked me why on earth I wanted to hurry with the work. "I am here," he said, "to see that you work these six hours you have been appointed to, but how the work is done and what is the amount of it does not concern me in the least, so why should it bother you? It is not our business." I think this is rather typical of Siberian land work.

One more funny detail to close this pretty description. Washing oneself in Siberia was certainly a highly complicated problem. But the washing of clothes often became a semi-tragical operation. To begin with, the co-operative shop scarcely ever had any soap, and bartering your best clothes seldom did any good, because really nobody in the village could get any soap for a fortune. But when, even by some miraculous good luck, I had got a piece, there remained the question of hot water, some sort of tub or bath to do the washing in, and a clothes rubber. Most of the time not one of these articles was available. The only way which remained to proceed with my washing was to walk with the dirty clothes straight into the pond or river (somehow it always happened so that my hut was within some few hundred yards or either one or the other) and there, taking an often involuntary bath, I scrubbed the things in this cold and dubiously clean water as hard as

I could. I must confess that in spite of all my efforts, the results of this laundry work were very unsatisfactory.

I am sorry to have given you a rather sad picture of the Russia of to-day, but unfortunately it is an absolutely true one. It would be a deep misunderstanding to think that I purposely want to represent the Russians as a particularly wicked or cruel people. Nothing is farther from my thoughts, and, on the contrary, I should like to impress upon my auditors that personally I have no complaint against the Soviet authorities, with which I never had any trouble. As for the people in Siberia, I became quite friendly with several of them, and they were indeed quite kind and human to me. What I think is that they are probably neither better nor worse than most nations of the world. But one thing is certain: that they are the poorest and the most unhappy people of this globe. *(Applause.)*

MR. HUDDART: [HUBBARD?] I believe I was put down to speak a few words after Countess Czarowska. I do not know why. I cannot add anything to what she has said. It was a most lucid and interesting description of life in Kazakstan. In retrospect I should think it will be a great memory of hers, when she has forgotten the privations she had to undergo in facing life in the raw. But I think there is one thing we ought to realize, and that is that her description of this must not be taken as absolutely typical of collective farms in Russia. There are some good ones and some bad ones. In the Steppes of Kazakstan agriculture is still a comparatively new industry. Until the last generation it was mere steppe land, covered by nomad hordes. It can hardly be expected that the standard of living for the farmers can be as high as it is in the famous wheat regions of European Russia. There are poor and primitive collective farms in Russia, or rather in the U.S.S.R., because I always try to distinguish between Asiatic and European Russia. It should be realized that the descriptions of happy collective farmers dancing in the streets to the sound of the accordion after their day's work may apply in some parts, but they do not apply everywhere. Sometimes I think there is a tendency for propaganda to concentrate on the more favourable aspects of conditions in Russia and to ignore the seamy side. I do not want to try to make out that Russia is a country where conditions are appallingly bad, but I do think a little corrective to the sometimes over-optimistic things that are spread about is useful.

There is one thing that struck me after I heard what Countess Czarkowska had to say. I have heard her talk a great deal about it, because I spent four weeks in the ship with her coming back from Russia, so I got the story first hand and in great detail. It is that it is the sort of life that has made the Russian soldier very tough, and that is how he has been able to go through this winter and stand conditions that the Germans have found intolerable. I think that is all I have to say, except that I congratulate Countess Czarkowska on the very lucid and interesting lecture she has given us. *(Applause.)*

THE CHAIRMAN: I think I may now on your behalf, and I know with your very fullest assent thank the Countess for her most interesting lecture. We have listened to lectures and addresses of many kinds here, some of them actually dealing with historical, others with political, others with different aspects of life. They all have their value. The supreme value of the address we have heard to-day is that it is a human picture, a piece of human life, of the type of which we see so little, of things which to us perhaps are almost unimaginable. It has held our interest, I know, from the very beginning. The impression I shall carry away is this, that the Countess did not come here to give us, as she said, a picture of Russia. She did not ask us to draw any conclusions about the state of Russian society or workers in Russia as a whole. It was a true picture of personal experiences, of a type which we hope have come to very few people, experiences which called for great patience, great endurance, great courage. I could have listened, I felt, to the Countess telling us of what she endured there, and the things she saw there, for hours together, because she gave us the intimate details which make up so much of life and tell us so much about life, those details which seem to go right into the heart of things. I know that on your behalf I can express to her our sympathy for what she had to endure, and for all the many other cultured, well-educated and intelligent Polish people who have suffered in the same way, many of whom now are still suffering in Siberia, unable to return to their homes or unable to be brought back, as she happily has been brought back from those same terrible surroundings. Our sympathy goes to her and to them also, and also our congratulations go to her that she and her children and her husband have been able to come here and see a happier side of life. I know that with that also our hopes will go that she and her many Polish friends may still see better days and a better world to live in. *(Applause.)*

Notes

1 Countess Sophia Hedwig Czarkowska-Golejewski, neé Sapieha-Rozenska (17 June 1900–6 November 1981). The Countess had one daughter, Rose, born in Lwow in 1933. We do not know who the other child was who went with her into exile. After the war the Countess was involved in a naturalisation dispute with the British Foreign Office. Papers from this dispute are closed until 2048. She died in London.

2 The NKVD was the Peoples' Commissariat for Internal Affairs, the Soviet

law enforcement agency, which replaced the GPU, the State Political Directorate.

3 Kazakhstan had become the Kazakh Soviet Socialist Republic in 1936, and was part of the Soviet Union.

4 With the seizure by Russia of eastern Poland, its inhabitants automatically became Soviet citizens.

German and Russian Armies

By General Sir Giffard le Quesne Martel
Lecture on 7 June 1944

Introduction

By the time this lecture was given, events were moving in favour of the Allied forces, although the war in Europe was to continue until 8 May 1945 and until September 1945 in the Far East. The day before the General's lecture had seen the D-Day landings on the French coast and the beginning of the liberation of Europe from the Nazis. Martel became Head of the British Military Mission to the Soviet Union in the Spring of 1943 and visited the front-line in the Kursk region, which was to be the site of a major battle which the German army lost. Part of the problem was the extremely long German front stretching from Leningrad in the north, which was under siege, to the Caucasus in the south, a distance of some 1,600 miles. Operation Barbarossa, the initial German launch into Russia, had failed, but Hitler was not prepared to withdraw.

Martel had been recalled from the Soviet Union at the beginning of 1944 and returned to Britain. His lecture shows both his skill as a tactician in warfare and his admiration for the Russian soldiers. Looking ahead, he said 'we [i.e. Britain] have to get on with the Russians after the war' – a view not shared by everyone including the newly appointed anti-Communist Head of the RAF, Sir John Babington.

The battle for Stalingrad, which lasted five months and is said to have cost two million lives, was the strategically decisive turning point in the German invasion of Russia. The Nazis were defeated by a combination of another bitter winter, weak support from other Axis armies and tenacious defence by the Russians. Martel discussed why the Russian army, in spite of much less sophisticated weaponry, was able to match German initiatives with other weapons, some of them psychological. He admired the Russian soldier: 'they are nearly all peasants, they never lose their way . . . they are very fine natural soldiers,' and had a gift for improvisation.

Martel forecast that at the end of the war the Russians would march into Germany, which is what in fact happened, East Germany being maintained as a Soviet satellite until re-unification in 1990. He also said that the Russian 'will put curtains up all round his country and try terribly hard to build up the standard of living', anticipating the Iron Curtain that was to divide Europe for more than four decades.

ROYAL CENTRAL ASIAN SOCIETY
Report of a Meeting held at Burlington House
on 7th June, 1944
Chairman: General Sir John Shea
Speech by General Sir Fiffard Le Quesne Martel[1]
Transcript from the Shorthand Notes of Charles Grouse,
Deputy for The Herriot Bureau, 145 Oxford Street, London W1

THE CHAIRMAN: Ladies and gentlemen, General Martel, who is going to speak to us to-day, has had a very distinguished career in the Army. He was, among other things, Deputy Director of Mechanisation at the War Office and Commander of the Royal Armoured Corps, but what is even far more important is the fact that to nobody does the Army owe so much for the evolution of the tank as to the lecturer to-day *(applause)* – and if you really want to know what a tank is like and what a tank does you should read a classic which he wrote, entitled *In the Wake of the Tank*. If you will forgive me for one moment for giving you a personal impression, I have never forgotten the effect the lecturer had on me in the days of cavalry. Fourteen years ago General Martel gave a lecture pointing out that at last in the fast-moving tank, cavalry had found the weapon that it wanted to accompany it. Then a year ago he was given that very difficult and important post at the head of the British Military Mission in Russia.

I am sure you will agree with me that there is nobody who is more qualified to tell us today about the operations that took place in Russia. General Martel.

GENERAL MARTEL: Ladies and gentlemen, what I have to do today is to run, rather briefly, through the whole of the operations in Russia, and then I shall dwell on various matters which I think will interest you most. In doing this, I shall touch at times on the psychology of the Russians. I shall make no excuse for doing that. We have to get on with the Russians after the war, and it is necessary for us to get all the knowledge we can of the psychology of the Russians. Taking it on the

The German Front in Russia, 1941 (Graphics: Jane Booker Nielsen)

whole, the lecture will be complimentary, after their success; and where it is not so complimentary, I think it is right I should tell you I do not think the Russian in the least minds, that he likes plain speaking, and I think the way to get on with him is to understand his good points and his bad points and be quite open with him.

This great campaign started by the Germans, as you know, breaking their pact with Russia and advancing with that magnificent army of theirs into Russian territory. Not a very big army as armies go. On the Russian front, some 170 divisions, equipped with everything they could possibly want, very highly trained. They had won two campaigns, one against Poland and another against France, and of course they were far ahead of anything the Russians had produced, in that short time, to put up against them.

This very fine, magnificent, German Army attacked, as you remember, on the Russian front, a narrow front, biting deeply into Russian territory and cutting off great parts of the Russian Army. The whole German plan was to smash the Red Army and not bother about territory or fronts or anything of that sort. In those thrusts they used their mechanised and armoured forces. Of course, the Russians had very heavy casualties, but something about them did just succeed, on several occasions, in enabling them to escape and save quite a large part of the Russian Army by the skin of their teeth at the last moment; and the reason why they could do that was their astonishing strength. Speaking of the Russian soldier, some of those who escaped at the last moment, in these pincer movements, must have marched an incredible number of miles a day. They carry a very heavy load, but in spite of this the Russian divisions did magnificent marching, and escaped to a large extent.

Then the Germans went on, as you remember, and got nearly up to Moscow. Then the winter set in. They had started their campaign rather late. The Germans said "All right, we will dig in on this line, 40 or 50 miles West of Moscow, and that will be our winter quarters," and their plan was to smash the Russian Army in the summer of 1942. That was their plan. But the Russians put on a very fine winter campaign, which hit the Germans very hard. At 30 degrees to 40 degrees below zero the Russians can fight perfectly well, but the German cannot handle his equipment at all. The Germans succeeded in stabilising the position that winter, and they were ready for the summer campaign of 1942. In that second summer offensive, he continued, as you remember, south of Moscow, and made great headway. He made deep thrusts into the enemy positions on the southern front that did not altogether succeed, so he went on with his armoured forces, on a narrow front, followed by large forces behind.

This met with great success. The position was extremely critical from the Russian point of view. Exactly what happened, we do not know. Marshal Stalin went out there with his Chief of Staff. There was a very considerable purge. Some 13 or 14 senior commanders disappeared,[2] and after that the Russians fought very well, and they slowed up the Germans quite considerably.

However, the Germans were still getting on. They had got to Stalingrad,[3] and they had got down to the Caucasus. At this stage we got very concerned, because if they succeeded in getting through the Caucasus down to Persia and into the Persian oilfields, they were the only oilfields that could supply us with oil from the Middle East. It was very critical from our point of view, so we made an Anglo-American plan, which was to have a very powerful air force – fighters, light bombers, medium bombers, and a great quantity of transport to supply them – and said to the Russians "Can we place this force on your soil North of the Caucasus? That will be the spearhead for our advance troops to protect our vital interests in Persia." The Russians thought about this for two or three weeks, and in the end said they could not allow this great body of foreigners to come on to their soil, but they would be very pleased to have the aeroplanes and the transport. I tell you that story, to show you the mentality of the Russians. The situation was really desperate from their point of view. The Germans were in Stalingrad and had got to the Caucasus. Even under those conditions the Russians would not do it. The Russian hates a large body of foreigners on his soil.

We could not give them this large amount of transport, to be used by them; they, naturally, had to be used by our own people. However, the German offensive down to the Caucasus came to a standstill, and winter was coming on. Now, in that autumn of 1942 that was the position. The Germans were stretched on a very long front from Leningrad down to the Caucasus, and had, of course, very long lines of communication down to Germany. Winter was coming on. They could not do offensive operations. They knew the Russians might do offensive operations, which they would have great difficulty in holding. What should the Germans have done? They should have withdrawn to a much shorter line West of Moscow, and if they had done that they might have saved their resources. At that time they had a large quantity of mechanical transport. They could have extricated them very easily at this stage and would have been set for their attempt to smash the Red Army in 1943.

Hitler, we believe, overruled his General Staff, and would not cede an inch of territory. This magnificent German Army, to start with a comparatively small army, had now been watered down to a larger and less efficient army to hold this huge front. That was really the turning point of the war. It was turned into a watered-down army of many more divisions, to hold that front. That winter the Russians put in a very fine counter-offensive and, launching armoured forces north and south of Stalingrad, beat up large parts of the German Army. I have no time to go into it now, but it brings out a great many interesting points. The Russians said "We will go in pursuit. We will organise our two armoured forces into two echelons; the first one will get behind the enemy, and the second one will try and get further behind the enemy. That was a simple and obvious plan, one which we might have used in North Africa on many occasions.

Another interesting point in the winter of 1942–1943 is this. The Russians were very short of transport. They started the war short of transport, and used it up in these great retreats and advancing again. They worked out their bare minimum essential, and found they only had transport to carry one-third of the bare minimum transport and food. The Russians said "We will take a third and capture the remaining two-thirds from the enemy." I do not know how many marks they would get for that from the Staff College. They worked it out very carefully. They studied the location of the German dumps. It was all carefully worked out beforehand. I have been all over the ground with the Russians. They show you this naturally with great pleasure and delight. It is only right they should do so; and I do not think the Russians were short of any petrol or food during those operations. It was a very brave act on their part launching those operations during the winter.

The Germans were thrust back to a line West of Moscow, and the Russians had to follow up. Then the thaw of 1943 set in. At that time our Chiefs of Staff were very concerned, because we had no information from Russia at all. Here was a very important stage in the war, and there was a Military Mission there all those years, and it had been boycotted by the Russians, and the Russians had allowed its members to see nothing and really treated them in a disgraceful way although representatives of their Allies. It was at that stage in the Spring of 1943, that the C.I.G.S.[4] told me I had to go out. I did not feel very pleased about it, but you can imagine one had to see if one could do something.

I asked advice, and found the policy had been, very naturally, to be nice to the Russians, pleasant, and so on; and this had produced nothing at all. Then I asked the younger representatives in the Foreign Office. I said "Have you any suggestions to make?" I said "We are, after all, all one team, we are allies, what can we do?" They said "There is only one way, and that is to be rather tough with the

Russians." It is quite easy to say be very tough with a chap, but when you come to do it, it is not very easy, it is not our outlook on life.

However, it was important we should get in touch with them. At this stage the Chiefs of Staff in this country did not know what state the Russian Army was in. Would it be able to face another campaign against the Germans? What state was the German Army in? On all these important matters our Chiefs of Staff were completely ignorant.

Anyway, off I went to Russia. I asked to see the front, and I was told I could see the front. The Mission had been out before, and been told something and seen nothing, so I was on the look out. I saw Marshal Malinovsky, Commander of the Southern front, and went to his head-quarters on the Donetz. I was shown in. The Commander had a map in front of him, one half covered with a sheet of paper, the other half had dispositions on. He told me the German dispositions in great detail. I said "Now I want you to tell me of the Russian dispositions." He looked at me and said "We never tell anybody anything about the Russian positions." So I simulated great anger. I said "Do you think I have come all the way out from England to be told that?" I pushed my face close to his. I was really in a terrible funk. (*Laughter.*) I expected he would send me back. He got crimson in the face, looked at me, and then he said "There you are, there is the whole thing." These Russians like plain speaking. So I cashed in on that. I said "Can I go up and see your positions at the front?" That enabled the Mission, for the first time in this war, to really get to know the Russian Army. We saw everything and were told everything and went about among them.

Now, I think, for a few moments I may tell you something about the Russian Army. One has to appreciate that the Russian Army is only about 20 years old, but the astonishing part is what a fine army they have produced in such a short time. It has plenty of failings, natural in a hastily trained army, but many good points as well. The first thing to talk about is the personnel. If you have not the right chaps, you cannot do anything. I went to Russia in 1936 to see their manoeuvres, and spent some time with them. At this time the officer was a frightfully weak link in the Russian Army. They had liquidated their officers from the Czarist regime. On manoeuvres you could stroll round and talk to a company commander who was about to launch an attack, and say "How are you going to launch your company?" and all he could do was to stand at attention and quote from the book, he had no confidence in himself at all. The Russians realised that, and started schools to bring up officers into the type of the officer class. When I was on the Donetz I had an opportunity of talking to them and seeing them, and I have no doubt the officer class is very good indeed. They talk to the men, and talk very nicely. The men listen to them, and the men are proud to serve their officers. That is undoubtedly so in the Russian Army. The Divisional Corps Commanders are very good, and the higher direction has been extremely good. I saw a lot of it when I was in Russia.

A word or two about the men. The men are the finest soldiers you could find anywhere in the world. I have already mentioned their strength, and I saw lots more of that when I got to the front. On one occasion they were short of ammunition – they were always short of transport. A man already carries 130 lbs. on his back – and they put a couple of 25-pounders on the back of each of a number of men. It was springtime and there was very deep mud – and off they went. If you put that on one of our chaps, he would just disappear in the mud. Their strength in that way is quite astonishing. As a soldier he is extremely good. They are nearly all peasants, they never lose their way, they hide themselves well; they are very fine natural soldiers. If you took one Russian soldier and put him against one German soldier, the Russian would win all the time. He is nearer the animal. But if you took one Russian unit and one German unit, equipped as the Germans were at the beginning of the war, the Russians had not a hope. The German technique is far ahead of the Russian technique; it is inevitable.

Now, a word about the equipment side; that is the next most important thing. The Russians, of course, in addition to raising their Red Army after the Civil War, had to industrialise their country to produce ammunition, – it is very difficult in an agricultural country like Russia – and they had foresight in putting those industries right away in the Urals. The Russian concentrated on essentials; he concentrated on guns, machine guns, and tanks. He made very good machine guns and fairly good tanks, and made those in considerable numbers. He made a very simple form of design. The army was very well equipped but when it came to refinements, scout cars, trucks, and that sort of thing, he rather skimped on those things – wireless trucks, and so on. He had a certain number which he used in the army at the beginning of the war, but they soon got worn out, and he was unable to replace them. They had bare essentials, but no refinements. Without refinements it is impossible to raise an army to a high state of technique.

At one time I went to see an armoured brigade just behind the front. The Commander said. "I am going to make that attack in this way." I said "How are you going to send the orders?" He said "I am going to send a marked map. I am going to use these tanks." I said "Are you?" He said "I have nothing else." He said "I know you have 14 special small vehicles with every armoured regiment on purpose for this sort of thing, but we have not got that. We cannot ask you to send us those, because of the shipping."

Therefore you find the Russian Army had a lower standard of technique from that point of view. That is why I told you earlier if you took two units of the same strength, equipped in that way, at the start of the war, one German and one Russian, the Russians had no chance at all. The organisation is very wonderful on the Russian side, but it is not very skilled or worked out in any great detail. In the Russian Army they accept a rather lower standard. For instance, one day they were reinforcing part of the front, and as the units were marching up this road they got mixed in with other units. We should be awfully upset to get someone else mixed in with one's own unit, but the Russians do not mind that. The first things to arrive were 10 tanks. As far as I could make out they were mostly from different units. The Staff Officer said "These are your 10 tanks, and off you go," and he took them. If you said that to a British officer, he would say, "But where is the regimental head-quarters?" and so on. But the Russians do not worry about those things. There are a good few days when food does not arrive. They are quite used to eating an enormous amount one day and digesting it during the next two or three days, and it seems to work very well.

You may say that is a bit critical of the Russians, but I do not think the Russian objects to that description of his army. It has done wonderful things, and that is the true position as I saw it.

Now, having seen the Red Army and sized it up a bit, I went back to Moscow and asked for meetings with the Russian General Staff. It was now half-way through May and June. The ground was drying up. It was the turning point of the war, and what was going to happen? I said as head of the British Military Mission I wanted to have a discussion with the Russian General Staff. They said "We do not discuss these matters," so I had to be rude to them and we got together very well. We had three meetings a week, and we discussed everything quite openly. What was passing through their minds they were quite prepared to discuss with you. I gathered they were going to initiate offensive operations against the Germans in the summer, June or July 1943. At that time the Germans had 20 first-class Panzer Divisions on that front. They had others as well. I had seen the Russian Armoured Corps, they could not compete with those German Armoured Divisions. The German Armoured Divisions I knew only too well. So when the Russians said "We are going to initiate offensive operations," I said "You poor boobs, I am sorry for you, you will be hit for six." They were very insulted, and off they went; and the next day they said will I have another talk. I came back, and they said "About this discussion the other day, what used you to do in those conditions in North Africa?" I told them under those conditions in North Africa we always sat back on the defensive and got the enemy to blunt his armoured forces against our strong defence, and then you can initiate the counter offensive and get him on the hop. We talked about this for a long time, and off they went again. Then they said would I come back the day after. We came back again and had another discussion. They said "We are very interested in the discussions we had a few days ago, but when they remained on the offensive the previous summer and the Russians were on the defensive, they did not blunt their armour against the Russian defence; the Germans went through a couple of hundred miles. How did you hold them up?" We discussed all that.

When the German attacks it is usually on a narrow front, about eight miles, with the support of low-flying aircraft, and he then turns and widens the gap. You cannot stop him breaking through. Our technique was to rush up reinforcements and hold the haunches each side of the break-through.

We discussed all these things with the Russians, and we found that the scheme for defence in depth of the Russians was extremely good, but they had not altogether appreciated the importance of holding the haunches as the first step when the Germans broke through. At the next meetings, at the start, the Russian officer present used to get up and say he wanted to make quite clear that holding the haunches had always been strongly stressed in the Russian regulations.

Finally came the day when the Germans did attack. The Russians decided to hold back, and it became quite clear the Germans were going to attack the Kursk salient, massing enormous panzer armies north and south of them. The Russians had their defence in depth very well laid out, and finally the Germans attacked on the 5th July, and from the north the mass of the armoured forces was held up by the defence in depth of the Russians. In the south the attack from Bielgorod made good headway. I said "They are getting through you a bit there." They said "We are rushing up reinforcements to hold the haunches", and after a few days they started pushing in from the haunches. So the attack made by the Germans on the Kursk salient completely failed.

The Russians launched a counter offensive. They chose the moment very well indeed, on the 12th July, at a stage when the maximum number of German divisions had been committed to the battle, some of them very badly hammered, their idea being to cut off the Oryol[5] salient. They started off very well, and they tried to cut the communications leading to Oryol. They went 30 or 40 miles in three or four days. If they had cut those communications a very large German force would have been cut off; but the Germans extricated panzer divisions and sent them there, and the panzers surrounded the armoured corps of the Russians at Oryol and the Russians did not move another inch.

Then the Russians said "We must start an attrition process all up and down the front." They were superior in strength to the Germans and were able to do that. That made the Germans send panzer forces up and down the front to try and meet those attacks, and by the 4th August the Russians thought the time had come when they should have another attack at the German forces, and this time they went for Kharkoff. They brushed aside the panzer divisions, but unfortunately, about the seventh day, the Germans extricated the 88 Panzer Corps from the south, and this got all round the Russian Armoured Corps and held them completely. So the Russians said "We can beat him by hammering him up and down the front," and so they continued the process up and down the front. This went on until the end of August. At the end of August the Russian said "The German is now too weak to hold his front," and then launched three great offensives simultaneously. The Germans had not enough armoured forces to begin to stop three offensives of that sort, and they began to fall back about two miles a day in front of these great forces. By this time the Russians on the front were three times the strength of the Germans in men, guns, and tanks. That is a tremendous lot. By that time you hardly ever saw a German plane on the Russian front. That was the position.

I do not want to detract for a moment from the very tough show the Russians did – their judgment and direction at the top was magnificent – but they had very great material advantage. They had strength everywhere, and that is an enormous advantage. They pushed on and got to the Dnieper, and then everybody said "The Russians will be held up for a very long time. The Russian communications are now very long, and we shall have a very long pause." But the Russian is much too good a soldier to give the Germans a chance to recover. Once he got to the Dnieper, he pushed across at once. The German was, by this time, getting very weak. In addition to that, the German Army had been very much affected by air bombardment. They were getting very short of equipment, short of tanks, and so on, partly due to the flow of munitions, but also due to the fact that their manufacture had been affected by our air bombardment. The Russians pushed on in a very wonderful way. The way they improvise is quite wonderful. You see Russians arrive with heavy axes. The officers, and one or two N.C.O.s,[6] push off in rubber boats and measure the depth of the river. They make sketches. They go off into the woods, and then they come back with timber felled from the local trees, and they may produce in three days a bridge to take 10-ton lorries. That is a very fine feat. We can bridge in half that time, but that depends upon getting the stuff up. They are very good at improvising. Both sides are very good at the railways, they have changed the gauge so often from one to the other.

From then, they never looked back. They pushed on right beyond the Dnieper, and finally down to the Carpathians, down to the present line.

Now the first point I think you would like me to talk about is this question of communications. How do the Russians keep going with these long communications? The answer is, the distance has not been quite so long as one would have imagined. If the Russian makes an attack somewhere, nothing comes out in the papers at all for about four or five days, then he announces "Quite recently an offensive started" somewhere. Actually, the speed is not quite as great as all that. The Russian is quite right in holding back his news, because he wants to see if it is going to be successful or not. In that way one gets a picture of a tremendous speed of advance, but if you work it out on your maps you will find the speed is two miles a day. Our advance in North Africa was 14 miles a day, and our distance of advance was more than twice the maximum distance of the Russians' advance. Those are the figures.

Then another question which I know you will want to ask is "What is the Russian going to do; is he going to go into Germany, or clear his own soil, or what?" I do not think there is any doubt about that at all. The Russian has, quite rightly, produced tremendous hate against the German in his country. He has had to do that, because the Russian is a very kindly chap; they do not naturally hate. The Germans have given them a number of perfectly true atrocity stories, but, in addition, the Russians have manufactured some. Why should not they? All that made an intense feeling of hate against the Germans, which is kept up all the time, and they are determined to get their own back.

In addition to that, there is the destruction by the Germans, which on the Russian soil has been quite tremendous. There were very few peasants who destroyed their own farms, but when the German came to withdraw, which he did at two miles a day speed, the German destroyed nearly everything. In 1500 miles there is hardly a house left. That sort of destruction is terrific, and the Russians are quite determined that the Germans are going to put that right, and they are going to make the Germans work as slaves after the war, and they are quite determined to march into Germany. They distrust us a little. They think we are going to be weak towards the Germans, and they are going to have that put right and see they never have the risk of fighting Germany again. *(Loud applause.)*

(The Chairman then introduced the following speakers.)

COLONEL MONKHOUSE: Mr. Chairman, ladies and gentlemen, I am afraid I did not know I was going to be called upon to say anything. I was very pleased indeed to listen to this most interesting talk we have had today from General Martel. There is only one question I should like to ask, and that is with reference to the last remark you made. You said when the Germans retreated across Russia they destroyed pretty well everything as they had gone. Have they destroyed all the industrial equipment, the mines and works and factories? I should be interested to know to what extent those things have been put out of action.

Thank you for asking me to speak, but I am afraid I cannot say anything more about this most interesting talk we have had.

GENERAL MARTEL: By and large, the Germans destroyed everything. There were places here and there where they got rushed on a bit faster than they intended to be, and they did not have time to destroy everything, but by and large they destroyed everything.

MR. ANDREWS: It is very kind of you to allow me to put a question. I do not speak as an expert at all, but one question rose to my mind as I was listening, and it is this: You explained to us the secretiveness of the Russian. One gathers from other sources that it is likely they will make, after the war, at least as much difficulty as they did before the war for their own people to travel and to get standards of comparison. One also gathers it is extremely difficult for me, from this country, to have any kind of contact other than official contact.

Now, taking those two together as two aspects of the same attitude of mind, I am wondering whether you would take it that those other sources were more or less correct; and, if so, whether that does not make it extremely difficult for the two countries to understand one another? Because if I am told that my opposite number is only to have official business contact with me it is very difficult to build up the imponderables.

GENERAL MARTEL: I think those suggestions are perfectly correct. The Russian is very sensitive. He might have some sort of inferiority complex in some way. He was keen before the war broke out to build up a standard of living in Russia similar to that of Europe. The standard of living was rising quite a bit before this war broke out. If war had not broken out I think the Russian would have been quite willing to allow unofficial contacts. This war has put everything right back, and the standard of living now in Russia is terribly low. I should say at the end of this war the Russian will put curtains up all round his country and try terribly hard to build up the standard of living.

MR. MARSHALL: Mr. Chairman, ladies and gentlemen, I am sure we have listened with a great deal of interest to General Martel. I think our thanks are due to him, as a nation, for the way he has appreciated Russian psychology. Before he did that, there was considerable difficulty in getting information out of the Russians.

With regard to the information asked for by the last speaker, there was always more difficulty in getting into Russia than into most other countries in the world. The position with regard to going into Russia today is more difficult, but I think in eight or 10 years, if it had not been for the war, it would have become much easier.

There are one or two questions I should like to ask you: To what extent our supplies of munitions to Russia were of use to Russia in finally repelling the Germans from Russian territory?

Another question: You mentioned tanks, certain classes of motor transport, armoured cars, and so on. You did not mention aeroplanes. I always had the impression that Russia had devoted a very great deal of attention to the development of the aeroplane industry and that they had made fairly considerable progress on the air side.

You mentioned the change of gauge in her railways which had taken place. In the last war the same thing took place. The Germans finally got over the difficulty by so arranging things that it could no longer be drawn again to the Russian gauge. It resulted, after the last war, in a certain number of lines remaining to German gauge.

I should like to conclude by thanking you very much indeed.

GENERAL MARTEL: The first question was, to what extent the Russians had used the munitions which we sent them. The main thing we sent to Russia, which has helped them most tremendously, has been transport, mostly American trucks, and food. They have been of the utmost value to the Russians. Without trucks and American transport the Russians would have been unable to carry on the war at all. We have sent tanks and guns, but not in the same class as food and the trucks.

The next point is about the air force. I meant to touch on the air force, but I got carried away with the story of the operations. The Russian air force is entirely used for army co-operation, nothing else. The reason for that is Russian technique in the air is a bit low, They have had to build it up in a very short time. When you fly in Russian planes the pilot follows the ground, like we used to do 15 to 20 years ago. The pilot is extremely good, but he will not fly you anywhere unless he can see the ground all the way. This very long range strategic bombing is beyond him. He concentrates on support of the Army, fights with the Army, and that he does extremely well.

MR. ASTON: In 1936 the Russians shot all their Generals and most of their trained Staff Officers. Has that proved to be an advantage or a handicap? Secondly, do the Russians seem to have any intentions on Persia after the war?

GENERAL MARTEL: As regards, the Generals, I think they were very definitely handicapped: men like Tukhachevsky,[7] who was a very fine officer indeed. They have replaced them all, but it must have been a handicap.

As regards Persia, I do not think Russia has any desire to seize any territory that has not got Russians on its soil. No doubt she will want one or two warm-water ports, but I do not think she wants to seize any territory that is not Russian.

Then there is a question about railways. The destruction of sleepers is a thing the Germans do very thoroughly. They have special machines to do it. But the Russians have overcome that and they do pretty well.

A SPEAKER: I would like to ask, in connection with the last remark, if you have any idea whether the Russians have any intentions in Central Asia?

GENERAL MARTEL: I am afraid I have no knowledge of that subject. I should think the same rules apply.

ANOTHER SPEAKER: I should like to ask whether Russia wants to acquire additional territory outside her boundary. Do you think she would want to acquire a sphere of influence outside her territory?

GENERAL MARTEL: That is a very difficult question. The Russian likes being on these advisory commissions, and so on. That is a different thing from acquiring territory. He is rather pleased to be invited to be on these commissions, and so on, and he can do without acquiring territory.

ANOTHER SPEAKER: Might I ask General Martel this? Is any special kudos given for inventiveness, in the Russian Army? They seem to be amazingly inventive.

Another question is concerning bridges, on which the General is a very well-known authority. I wondered if they had any standardised bridges built for road and rail work, of good types, in even though they have not been able to use them very much.

GENERAL MARTEL: Quite a number of awards are given in the form of medals, which are awarded to inventors, and so on, and very highly prized, and I think that goes very well.

As regards the bridges, they have a certain amount, and they are very good at thinking out beforehand. Some of the bridges over the Dnieper they repaired very quickly.

As regards actual equipment, they are a long way behind us in the amount and the nature of their bridging equipment.

THE CHAIRMAN: I would like to ask you three questions, if I may.

One is: Where were the enormous reserves which the Russians produced for their counter offensives for the Stalingrad period?

The next question is: I understand there was a period when the Russian higher direction considered it was essential to enhance the prestige of the officer and stiffen the discipline of the Army.

The third question is: You told us the Russian soldier compared with the German soldier man to man was a better man, but that the Russian unit was inferior in technique to the German unit. Did that imply that when there was a clash of these very large forces the Russian losses were very big compared with the Germans'?

GENERAL MARTEL: The first question is where these troops were trained. I am afraid I cannot answer that, I am afraid I do not know. That was before I arrived in Russia.

On the question of raising the standards of discipline, that has been going on fairly continuously the whole time. Gradually they are going back to the Czarist days. The idea that now Russia is a classless society is complete bunkum; the officer is quite a different class from the men. Discipline in the Russian Army is very much like that in our Army, or any other army.

The last question, about the losses by the Russians. They were very very heavy in the first part, when they were trying to stand up to this magnificent German Army; and they were very heavy when they could not take Oryol and Kharkoff, which was a frontal attack; but when they had worn the Germans down by a process of attrition and attacked on a wide front, their losses were very much lighter. The Russian is a very able fellow. I do not think now he is suffering very heavy casualties at all.

THE CHAIRMAN: Ladies and gentlemen, I think that I have read everything that General Martel has published, and I always took a very deep interest in his career; but apart from his very marked ability, which I knew of, I wondered what the secret of his success was. I certainly have learned it to-day. It seems to me that, in combination with a delightful sense of humour, he can turn on the rough stuff at will, and smile immediately afterwards.

I do not think, sir, we can thank you enough for your most charming entertainment, and for your real instruction. Thank you very much. *(Loud applause.)*

Notes

1 General Sir Giffard Le Quesne Martel, KCB, KBE, DSO, MC (10 October 1889–3 September 1958) was a British Army officer who served in both World War One and World War Two. He was an engineer and had a practical interest in the construction of the tank, and its role in warfare.

2 In fact numbers are estimated to have been considerably higher, perhaps as many as 300 officers.

3 Now Volgograd.

4 Chief of Imperial General Staff.

5 The town is also known as Orel. It was in German hands before the Russian offensive. The 'salient' refers to a bulge in the front line.

6 NCO – non-commissioned officer.

7 Mikhail Tukhachevsky, executed on Stalin's orders in June 1937.

Index